The Cleveland Circular

a cycle route around the North York Moors

The Cleveland Circular

a cycle route around the North York Moors

David Branson

Published by Sigma Leisure – an imprint of
Sigma Press, Stobart House, Pontyclerc, Penybanc Road, Ammanford, Carmarthenshire SA18 3HP.

British Library Cataloguing in Publication Data
A CIP record for this book is available from the British Library.

ISBN: 978-1-85058-963-1

Typesetting and Design by: Sigma Press, Ammanford.

Cover photographs: left to right: Stain Dale Water, Rosedale Iron Kilns, Robin Hoods Bay, Roseberry Topping; main picture: Rievaulx Abbey

Maps and photographs: David Branson and Clare Branson, unless otherwise stated

Printed by: TJ International Ltd

Disclaimer: the information in this book is given in good faith and is believed to be correct at the time of publication. No responsibility is accepted by either the author or publisher for errors or omissions, or for any loss or injury howsoever caused. Only you can judge your own fitness, competence and experience. Do not rely solely on sketch maps for nagivation: we strongly recommend the use of appropriate Ordnance Survey (or equivalent) maps.

Contents

Introduction

The Cleveland Circular is a cycle trail of nearly 125 miles, mainly off-road, which creates a route around the North York Moors National Park, including the Cleveland Hills, encompassing some of the most dramatic scenery in England. The route makes use of two abandoned railways now used as bridleways, these being the Scarborough to Whitby line, as well as the Rosedale Ironstone Railway. In addition, the route takes in the old drover's road along the top of the Hambleton Hills, from which it is possible to look across the Vale of York to the Yorkshire Dales in the west.

The route can easily be accessed by rail at a number of points, such as Battersby Junction, Thirsk, Pickering, Scarborough, Whitby and all the stations from there to Egton Bridge. It is a challenging route, which could be completed in two or three days, but which has been split into five more manageable sections of around 20 to 30 miles. I have used the large-scale Ordnance Survey Maps Explorer OL 26 and 27, and relevant points are indicated by reference to these maps. This is not a route to be completed at speed, nor is it designed as an endurance test. Instead, it is intended to provide a varied tour of the North York Moors to be enjoyed at leisure, and which I am sure will provide a lifetime of memories.

The route begins and ends at Lord Stones Café, located by the side of Carlton Bank (map ref. 523 030). This is a delightful stopping-place much frequented by cyclists and walkers. It is open nearly every day, and there is ample parking space if you are bringing the bike by car. However, if you want to come by train, you might wish to start at Clay Bank, which is about 3 miles away to the east, and easily reached from Battersby Junction.

The idea of creating a circular cycling route came to me after completing the Cleveland Way walk a few years ago. The Cleveland Way, with the Tabular Hills Link, is a complete circular route around the North York Moors, taking in many of the places which you come across in the Cleveland Circular. I was taken by the idea of a route which eventually came back to its starting point and covered most of the North York Moors. As it is a route for cyclists, it cannot follow the same route as the Cleveland Way, as parts of this route are not suitable for bikes. Moreover, I wanted to make use of the disused railways in the area, which provide such excellent off-road cycling. This is why the Cleveland Circular does not go to the coast like the Cleveland Way, but cuts across the moors along the line of the old Ironstone Railway between Ingleby Greenhow and Rosedale.

As such, the route includes too many highlights to mention here, but probably the most memorable are the view from the top of the incline at the end of the Rosedale Ironstone Railway, or the wide, wooded valley which rolls down to the hamlet of Hackness from the exit of Dalby Forest. Every leg of the route has its special treasures, and I am sure you will find them as delightful as I did. You can do the circuit in any direction, but for the best results I suggest you follow the itinerary as laid out below ... and have a great trip!

A word about the North York Moors

The North York Moors are the largest area of wild moorland in England and cover an area of approximately 554 square miles (or 1432 square kilometres). The moors rise to over 1300 feet (454 metres) on the north-western escarpment, before gradually falling away to the south and east. To the south-east of the escarpment, there are extensive areas of high moorland cut by a series of river valleys running south to the Vale of Pickering, including Rosedale, Farndale, Bransdale and Bilsdale. To the north-east of the high moorland, the Esk Dale valley runs eastward to the coast at Whitby, providing a main line of communication. A number of smaller valleys, such as Great Fryup Dale, Westerdale and Danby Dale, flow northwards into Esk Dale, where there is a single-track railway which runs to the coast.

The whole of the moors are criss-crossed by bridleways and minor roads, which provide innumerable routes for the hardy cyclist. In addition, there is a bridleway on the disused rail-track which runs across the moors from Rosedale to the escarpment near Ingleby Greenhow, before dropping precipitously down a one-in-five incline to the Cleveland Plain below. The moors are a veritable paradise for the mountain biker, with a wide variety of scenery, including wild moorland, gentle valleys and the dramatic cliff-side panoramas from the coastal paths in the east.

The moors themselves are also steeped in history. There are medieval religious houses at Rievaulx Abbey and Mount Grace Priory, only a short distance off the route, as well as the well-known abbey at Whitby. There are many old castles and churches, including substantial castles at Helmsley and Pickering, not forgetting the fascinating church at Lastingham with its Saxon crypt. Close to the route is the sedate splendour of Duncombe Park country house with its mock classical temples overlooking Rievaulx Abbey. Finally, the remnants of the early industrial age are to be found in the ironstone kilns at Rosedale, and the disused Rosedale Ironstone Railway itself, which snakes over the moors to the Tees valley.

The North York Moors are alive with a wide variety of flora and fauna – you just need to stop once in a while and look for them. If you do the circular in August, you will see the moors at their best, clad in purple heather for mile after mile. Mixed in with the heather, there are patches of bright green bilberry plants, which produce ripe purple fruit earlier in the summer. You will become familiar with the raucous call of the ever-present grouse, and the sight of the lapwing and golden plover. You may even be lucky enough to catch a glimpse of the elusive adder, Britain's only venomous snake, which will do its best to keep out of your way.

Overall, the North York Moors offer the traveller a wide selection of different experiences in a relatively small area. Dotted around, there are many different types of settlement, from bustling railway towns to quiet moorland villages, all with their own peculiar history. In addition, there are many natural features, such as craggy hilltops, precipitous cliffs and sleepy valleys, all of which go to make up the wide variety of the moors. Crossing the North York Moors by bike is an excellent way of getting to know the countryside and is truly exhilarating at times. It even makes up for those days when you find yourself pushing your bike up an impossibly steep hill in the driving rain, totally lost as the light fails – well, maybe!

Train at Grosmont Station

The North Yorkshire Moors Railway

One very useful means of communication in the North York Moors, is the locally run North Yorkshire Moors Railway (note that the term 'Yorkshire,' not 'York' is used here!). This runs from Pickering to Grosmont where it connects to the Esk Valley line operated by Northern Rail, which runs from Middlesbrough to Whitby. Together they provide an invaluable transport system, which links several key locations on the circular route. As it is possible to put your bike on the train, it can be used to get across the moors quickly to your starting point. In any case, a trip on the railway is a very rewarding experience and could be done on a day off – if you allow yourself one!

The North Yorkshire Moors Railway was constructed in 1836, to transport goods from the port of Whitby to the town of Pickering and other inland towns and villages of North Yorkshire. This was a considerable enterprise, involving the construction of nine timber bridges over the Esk and a tunnel through the hill outside Grosmont. The route from Grosmont to Goathland was too steep for the carriage to be pulled by horse, so a pulley system was set up, which used a huge tank of water to act as a counterweight to pull the loaded carriages up the slope.

For nearly ten years the route was used by horse-powered transport, but in 1845 the line was bought by the York & North Midland Railway Company, who upgraded the track so that it could be used by steam-powered locomotives. The wooden bridges on the route were replaced by stone ones, and a new, larger tunnel was constructed at Grosmont. The existing route up to Goathland was seen to be too steep for locomotives, so it was decided to construct an alternative route to the west of the line. This opened in 1865 and is known as the 'deviation route'. This is the route now used by the track, whilst the original route is part of a walkway beside the track called the 'Rail Trail', which runs from Grosmont to Goathland.

The rail link became part of a national rail network, especially after it was connected to the York to Scarborough line. As such, the line provided a key link between York, Scarborough and Teesside. However, in the 1960s the government decided to close many local lines, as they were no longer deemed to be profitable. This included the Pickering to Whitby line, although the link from Middlesbrough to Whitby was eventually retained. The result was that the Grosmont to Pickering section was forced to close in 1965.

Fortunately, a small group of enthusiasts formed a preservation society, which was able to re-open the Grosmont to Pickering route as a private venture. The first train ran along the newly re-opened section in February 1969, where it was greeted by a great crowd on its arrival at Grosmont. Since that time the North Yorkshire Moors Railway has gone from strength to strength, and now operates a regular service between Pickering and Whitby, often involving steam trains.

Structure of the Guide

For the purposes of clarity, I have separated the sections which provide route information from the sections providing more detailed information about the places you come across on the route. The route directions are in bold and the other information is in normal text. I have also provided a series of simple maps to illustrate each section of the route. Usually the places described will be en-route, but occasionally I mention places which are just off the route, but which would repay a quick visit. Obviously whether you go there is up to you, but if you use the route as a means to discover the North York Moors, then you may wish to spend that extra time heading off the main route to see what interesting places lie around the corner.

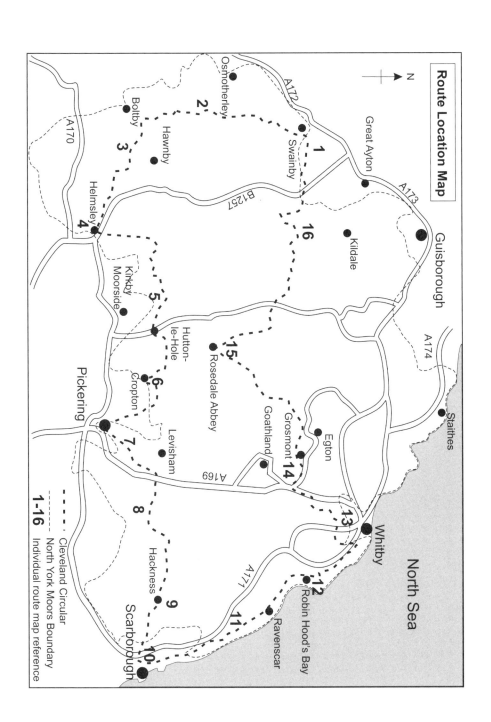

Acknowledgements

I would like to thank my wife, Marion, who spent many hours proof-reading the book as well as providing material on flora and fauna. I am also grateful to my daughter, Clare, who provided some of the photographs, and my son, Paul, who accompanied me on part of the route. Thanks are also due to my friend Andrew Wright who tested out part of the route and provided one of the photographs.

In addition, I would like to thank the many people I met on my travels who were so helpful and provided much interesting information. A special thanks should go to the North York Moors National Park staff, who gave me valuable information on whom to approach to obtain permission for publicising various parts of the route. I would also like to thank the various landowners who have been willing to allow access over their land, allowing us all to enjoy this magnificent countryside.

1: On the Hambleton Hills

Day 1	Lord Stones Café to Helmsley (Maps 1-3)
Distance	28 miles
Allow	5 hours
Terrain	Generally easy going with one long road ascent and a rocky path up to the Hambleton Hills
Toilets	Lord Stones Café, Swainby, Osmotherley (award-winning in fact!), Rievaulx Abbey and Helmsley
Refreshments	Lord Stones Café, Osmotherley, Rievaulx Abbey and Helmsley

In the shadow of the Cleveland Hills

The starting and finishing point of the route is Lord Stones Café, located on the col between Cringle Moor and Carlton Bank (523 030), and accessible from the minor road which connects Carlton in Cleveland and Chop Gate (pronounced Chop Yat!). The café is named after the nearby Three Lords' Stone, which marked the boundary between the lands of three local landowners, the Duncombes of Hemsley and Duncombe Hall, the Whartons of the Wharton Estate and the Dudley de L'isle family who owned extensive property in the area.

The café was built in 1989 and is open throughout the year. It serves a wide range of foods and is also licensed for the sale of alcohol. Lord Stones café is much frequented by mountain bikers, road cyclists and walkers and is an excellent place to start and finish the route.

The first stage begins with an exhilarating steep descent down Alum House Lane to Carlton in Cleveland, having turned right at

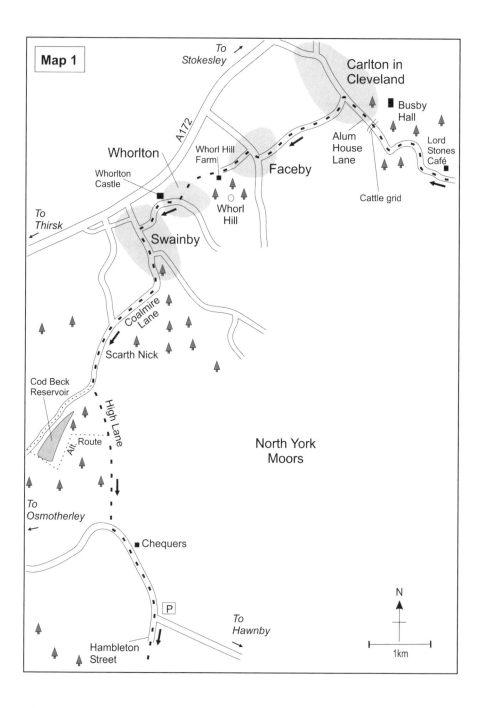

Map 1

To Stokesley

Carlton in Cleveland

Busby Hall

A172

Whorlton

Whorl Hill Farm

Faceby

Alum House Lane

Lord Stones Café

Whorlton Castle

To Thirsk

Whorl Hill

Cattle grid

Swainby

Coalmire Lane

Scarth Nick

Cod Beck Reservoir

High Lane

Alt. Route

North York Moors

To Osmotherley

Chequers

P

N

To Hawnby

Hambleton Street

1km

Lord Stones Café

the exit to the car park at Lord Stones (see Map 1). This an excellent way to 'psych' yourself up for what is quite a long ride ahead. At the junction before the entrance to the village there is another road leading off sharp left, which you cycle along for about ¾ mile to reach the village of Faceby. At the junction in Faceby, you bear right and then take the first turning off to the left, which is just before the end of the village.

This is a small lane, which runs up a slight hill past some farm buildings, until it reaches Whorl Hill Farm (492 030). At the farm, a sign indicates the route to Whorlton off to the right, although this is now very faded. I noted that there are some signs asking for cyclists to cycle quietly. You then need to go around the right-hand side of the farmhouse where you pick up the bridleway. This track leads across a couple of fields and you will see the spire of a church in the distance. The going is difficult here at first, with the route following a narrow path at times and the way being blocked by lots of mud if it has just rained. At times the path seems more like an obstacle course and it might be necessary to carry your bike sometimes – I certainly did!

However, after a few tricky manoeuvres, the track becomes easier to cycle and eventually leads onto a wide and well-worn farm track before arriving at a field. Bear right across the field to the gate almost opposite, where you join a tarmac road, with the church which you noticed before, virtually in front of you.

You turn right at the exit to the field, and cycle down the road past the imposing remains of Whorlton Castle.

The hamlet of Whorlton and village of Swainby lie just a mile apart from each other and their history is very much interlinked. The earlier settlement was at Whorlton, where there are the ruins of Whorlton Castle and the Church of the Holy Cross. The castle lies just to the right, down the hill from the junction with the bridleway, whilst the church lies just off to the left across the road.

The castle remains are those of the gatehouse erected in the late 14th-century by the D'Arcy Family. The original castle was a motte and bailey castle built on the impressive promontory of Whorlton Hill, with a commanding view over the plain below. This castle was ruinous by the mid-14th-century, when the village was hit by bubonic plague and abandoned. In the late 14th-century Sir Phillip Darcy constructed a tower-house and gatehouse linked to the original construction. The gatehouse still remains, as well as some of the vaulting of the now-demolished tower-house. The ruin is open to visitors at most times and is well worth a visit if time allows.

Whorlton Castle

Up the hill, there are the remains of the Church of the Holy Cross. The original church was built in the 12th-century to serve the village of Whorlton. However, when the plague decimated the village, the survivors moved down the hill to found a new settlement at Swainby. The church remained in use, but was now quite a way outside the new village. Eventually it was abandoned in 1875, when a new church was opened in Swainby. The site of Holy Cross church is very atmospheric, especially given its links to the deserted village of Whorlton. The original nave remains as two rows of arches open to the sky. However, towards the apse, part of the building has been reconstructed to provide shelter for the tombs of the local gentry buried within. This truncated church is used for services on special occasions. The churchyard outside holds the graves of many local people, who now lie buried on the hill overlooking Swainby.

Follow the road down the hill into Swainby, where you pass another church on your left, before crossing over a stream by way of a small stone bridge. Then, turn left and cycle through this pleasant, sleepy village. By this time, I found I was starting to get over the 'hassle' of the muddy bridleway and looking forward to the ride ahead with the Hambleton Hills beckoning.

The village of Swainby stands on Scugdale Beck with two roads running down either side of the watercourse and a little area of common land by the river itself. There are seats here and it is possible to sit and watch the world go by if you wish. The village was first referred to in around 1300, but it really began to develop in the 18th-century, when ironstone was discovered in the nearby Scugdale valley. In addition, it acted as an important staging post on the Drovers' Road over the Hambleton Hills. There is a shop in Swainby if you need to stock up with provisions for the journey, as there are no other stops until Rievaulx, unless you intend to divert to Osmotherley.

Climbing up to the Hambleton Hills

At the south end of the village, take the right-hand turning, which leads to Osmotherley. The road is called Coalmire Lane, and it winds slowly for ¾ mile up to Scarth Nick, where the road crosses over the top of the northern ridge of hills at a height of over 660 feet. This is also where the route first crosses the path of the Lyke Wake Walk, a gruelling 42-mile walk across the moors. This is the first real climb of the trip, and your legs begin to feel the strain as you approach the col on the ridge, having zigzagged all the way up the hill. However, after this tiring climb there is a reward by way of a fast descent down to the small reservoir at Cod Beck, a popular spot for day-trippers from Middlesbrough. More to the point, you

are now out of the Cleveland plain and into the Cleveland hills, with the Hambleton Hills only a short distance away!

Before you get to the reservoir, just where Coalmire Road swings round to the right, head straight on across the stream to a dirt track, which climbs up the hill on the other side. The stream is forded at this point, but the less adventurous can use the adjacent bridge. This dirt track is actually the beginning of High Lane, which is a track up the slope on the left side of the reservoir, skirting the adjacent wood (map ref 472 993). Initially this is rather hard going, and you may find it easier to push your bike up over the rough stone track. Later on, the track becomes easier to ride, and eventually turns into a tarmac road. Alternatively, you can cycle down Coal Mire Lane to the turn-off next to the reservoir dam, and then follow the cycle-track through the woods to meet up with the track. Although the second route is less direct, it does afford a dramatic view of the reservoir from the dam embankment.

It is also possible to divert to Osmotherley, if you require refreshments at this point. To get there, just continue down the road by the side of the reservoir, and it will take you straight there. The village of Osmotherley is not on the route itself but is only a short diversion from it. If you do decide to go there, you will then need to take the road south out of the village, which goes to Hawnby. This turns eastwards and rises up the hillside until it meets High Lane just before the farm at what was once Chequers café (474 971).

Osmotherley is a small village which nestles in the north-western corner of the North York Moors. The village has a good selection of pubs and cafés, one pub being the Queen Catherine, named after Catherine of Aragon who stayed in the area. It was the inability of Henry VIII to get a divorce from Catherine that was the starting point for the English Reformation.

The village was the scene of some of the early preaching by John Wesley at the so-called 'barter table' in the centre of the village, next to the village cross, which lies at the heart of the village by the main road junction. This eventually led to the building of the first ever Methodist chapel in 1754, which is located in Chapel Close. Just outside the village, up on Swinestye Hill, there is a Catholic Lady Chapel dedicated to the Assumption of Our Lady and St. Nicholas. This was once connected with the Carthusian priory at Mount Grace, when it was used as a hermitage, and after the dissolution of the monasteries as a place of pilgrimage. The chapel fell into disrepair in the 19th-century, but was restored in 1961 and is now used by the Benedictine monks of Ampleforth as a retreat, and by local Catholics for services.

The Carthusian Priory of Mount Grace itself is located at the foot of Mount Grace Wood, about two miles out of Osmotherley, accessible from the A19. It was founded in 1398 by Thomas de Holland and was very small and exclusive. In all, there was only a Prior and 23 monks, all of whom lived as hermits in their own cells grouped around the main cloister. The priory was one of the wealthiest in England at the time of its dissolution in 1539, when the property went to the Manners Family at Helmsley Castle. Whilst the priory is a little too far off the route for a quick visit, it might be possible to come back at a later date.

At the junction of High Lane and the road to Hawnby, you turn left and soon pass a farm called 'Chequers' (once a useful café but now, unfortunately, closed). Here the Hambleton Hills come into full view with their wooded, western slopes just visible. At last you start to see the climb ahead with its promise of a magnificent view when you reach the summit – of course that is the difficult bit!

The Chequers Farm was once an inn used by drovers on the Hambleton Drove road (see below). Outside the inn was a field enclosed by a stone

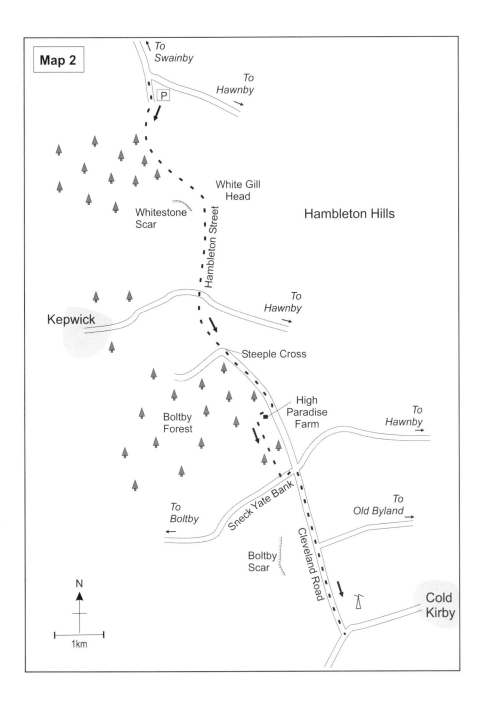

Map 2

To Swainby

To Hawnby

P

White Gill Head

Hambleton Hills

Whitestone Scar

Hambleton Street

Kepwick

To Hawnby

Steeple Cross

High Paradise Farm

To Hawnby

Boltby Forest

Sneck Yate Bank

To Boltby

To Old Byland

Cleveland Road

Boltby Scar

Cold Kirby

N

1km

wall, where the cattle could be kept overnight. The inn had a turf fire, which it was said had burnt continuously for over a hundred years. The inn later became a café but this is no longer open, which is a great pity, as it would provide one of the few places to obtain refreshments on this part of the route, other than diverting to Osmotherley.

You might notice an old chequer board attached to the front wall of the house which was once the old inn sign. This carries the mysterious ditty '... Be not in haste, stay and taste ale tomorrow for nothing'. I think the assumption is that tomorrow you may be dead and so will have no need to spend money.

The road runs on for nearly a mile to the car park where it turns off sharply to the left. At this point, you go straight on and pick up the track called Hambleton Street, which leads up towards the summits of the Hambleton Hills; the track has a sign saying 'no entry' to motor vehicles, so you cannot miss it (see Map 2). The route here starts easily enough, but gets gradually steeper and increasingly rocky and uneven. Only the fittest and most determined cyclist can get right to the top without dismounting. I was obviously not that fit or determined, and found it easier to push the bike up this stretch. However, once I reached the top it was great to rest for a while, and look out over the Vale of York stretching out before me, knowing that all of the hard climbing on this stage of the route was finally over.

Along the Hambleton Drove Road

The cycle route follows the course of the Hambleton Drove Road for the first part of its way along the Hambleton Hills. This is an ancient routeway which was used in the 18th-century by the cattle drovers, who brought their herds down from Scotland to the English markets. As many as 30,000 cattle each year were driven down to the south of England from Scotland following the Act of Union in 1707. The route went across the Hambleton Hills, starting from Swainby and climbing up Black Hambleton, eventually leaving the moors near Kilburn. The drovers preferred to use this route because it meant that they avoided the tolls on the turnpike roads below. In addition, they were able to prevent their cattle getting mixed up with those belonging to local farmers in the plains below. The drove roads were a key feature of the early industrial revolution period, before the arrival of the train made such methods of transport unnecessary.

Once you get to the top of the climb, the track becomes much more even, as we reach the plateau of the Hambleton Hills. Cycling now is a real pleasure, with some magnificent views over to the west, when not obscured by the dry-stone walls. The route runs along the top of the hills for over two miles, following the course of Hambleton Street, and there are occasional viewpoints such as at the junction with the road from Hawnby. At Steeple Cross (495 902) there is a slight deviation through the very edge of Boltby Forest for about ½ mile, before re-emerging at Dale Town Common. I found the forest track very easy going, especially as it was on a slight downhill slope and the track quite smooth. However, once you leave the forest, the route becomes a heavily-rutted track running along the open moorland. Eventually you come to a sign indicating a bridleway off to the right, leading towards High Paradise Farm (503 887), following the route of the Cleveland Way. This track may be missed if you cycle too fast, but you should note an information board opposite the turn which will help you to spot it.

You go down a short tree-lined track to the farm, but I noted that there were signs asking cyclists to dismount as they walked through the farmyard itself. After passing through the farm, the road becomes quite steep, and it is important not to overshoot the gate on the left, by a bend in the road, which is indicated as a bridleway. You go through the gate and take a grassy path which runs off across the field, and shortly reaches a gate leading into a wood. This is the introduction to an undulating ride down a well-marked path hugging the woodland slopes, with the sunlight trying to break through the tree cover (if you're lucky!). Apart from watching out to ensure I didn't slip over the edge, this was a very pleasant experience. After a short way you reach the tarmac road which goes down Sneck Yate Bank. At this point, turn sharp left up this road, and then right, to join Cleveland Road, which is indicated by a sign for Old Byland and Cold Kirby (510 877).

Descending into the Ryedale Valley

You continue south down Cleveland Road for two miles in an almost straight line, the route offering a wide vista over the Vale of York, and in the distance, the Vale of Pickering. You avoid the first turning off to Old Byland, but take the second turning off to the right indicated to Cold Kirby, just past a transmitter tower (see Map 3). The road now starts to go downhill, and you begin a long section of downhill 'free-wheeling'. At the entrance to Cold Kirby, you take the small road off left, signposted to Old Byland, which requires you to do a little more cycling. This soon turns sharp right and starts to go downhill again for just over a mile, until you reach Old Byland, the scene of a major battle between the English and Scots in 1322.

At the entrance to the village there are two bridleways off to the right; you need to take the first one just before the marker stone for Old Byland (548 857). This leads to a heavily-wooded valley, which must be cycled through with care, as there are steep slopes off to the left over the river. Once out of the wooded valley, you go through a gate and enter a series of open fields with a bridleway across. Just head opposite, and you will see the gate with the bridleway markings on the other side of the first field. In the second field, you follow along the left-hand edge down a long slope, which eventually leads you to another gate at the entrance to Callister Wood.

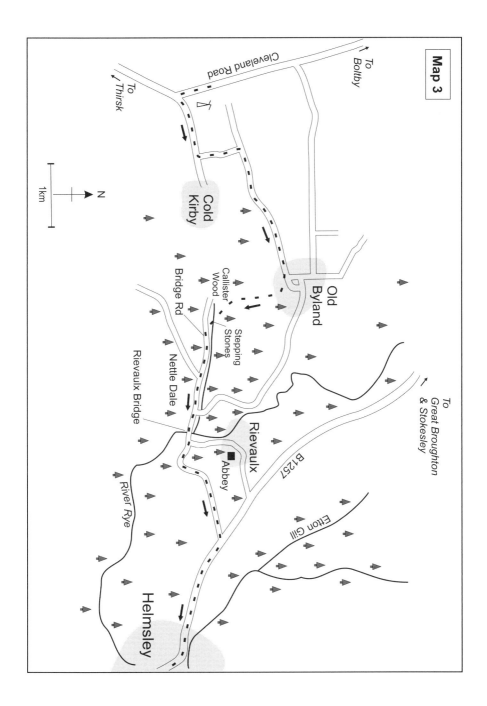

Map 3

To Boltby

Cleveland Road

To Thirsk

N
1km

Cold Kirby

Old Byland

Callister Wood

Bridge Rd

Stepping Stones

Nettle Dale

Rievaulx Bridge

Rievaulx

Abbey

B1257

To Great Broughton & Stokesley

River Rye

Elton Gill

Helmsley

27

Entering Callister Wood, you go down a steep slope, which must be negotiated with care as it quickly hits the roots of a tree and drops down a sharp bank. Keep straight on following the sign directing you to Nettledale, and you will see a small stream below on your right. The track is steep and narrow here and positively treacherous in muddy conditions; you might want to walk with the bike at this point. Finally you reach the stream, which can be crossed by way of a new concrete footbridge, before you cross the field to a stile at the far side, which you have to lift the bike over. At this point, head directly ahead and you will see a small waymarked path, which leads to a gate, beyond which the path crosses some stepping-stones to reach a track known as Bridge Road (555 846).

Turn left down Bridge Road, and you cycle past a series of small reservoirs and ponds, much frequented by anglers, as you enter the scenic valley of Nettledale. This is a delightful run, helped by the fact that the ride is coming to its end and the town of Helmsley is not too far away. Indeed, this track is also the route of the Cleveland Way as it leaves Helmsley to run up to Cold Kirby and onto the Hambleton Hills.

The track ends at a gate, where you turn left down the tarmac road, which runs for a mile eastwards through the dale towards Rievaulx Bridge (pronounced "Reeve-oh"). At the bridge, it is possible to see the outline of the magnificent Rievaulx Abbey, which can be visited if you take a detour up the road off to your left.

Nestling in the steep-sided Ryedale Valley, a few miles from Helmsley, Rievaulx Abbey was the first Cistercian Monastery to be built in England, and its impressive ruins are located in a very atmospheric spot. It was originally founded in 1131 as a Cistercian house by monks who had come across from France. The monks developed farming on a series of large farms or 'granges', where they raised flocks of sheep which were used to produce wool. Later on, they started the mining of ironstone, which they transported by means of a system of canals. The Abbey eventually became very wealthy, before it was finally closed down in the Reformation. The lands were then sold to the Manners family, who used the income they generated to fund the construction of their stately home at Duncombe Park.

Above the ruins of the abbey there is a man-made terrace on which are located two mock-classical temples built by the owners of Duncombe Park. The larger temple is square in shape, and has a dining room which was used for formal banquets, with a kitchen in the room underneath. The smaller temple is round in shape and of 'Tuscan' design. These are now in the care of the National Trust and can be glimpsed from the abbey below.

Rievaulx Abbey

Rievaulx Abbey is a delightful place to stop, and I would recommend that you take some time out of your trip to come here, and experience its tranquillity. At the same time you can sample the delights of the well-provisioned tea-room attached to the abbey, which can be visited without having to pay to go round the abbey itself. It is then possible sit outside and contemplate the view whilst taking refreshment, aware that you are nearly at the end of this challenging stretch of the route.

The cycle route continues straight on, and climbs through Abbot Hag Wood, before emerging onto the open land above. A ½-mile stretch then brings you to the junction with the B1257 road, which runs between Great Broughton and Helmsley, from which you can see the impressive country house of Duncombe Park. Turn right here and head down towards Helmsley.

There is a final stretch of 1½ miles along this road into Helmsley. This is one of the few parts of the circular route which follows a major road, but fortunately it is all downhill, and so it is a very quick run. In no time you reach Helmsley, where you take the first turning past the church to reach the market square, with its impressive town cross at the centre. This is the finish point for the first section of the route, and an opportunity to have a welcome drink at one of the many hostelries around the square.

Helmsley is one of the most delightful small towns you will encounter on the Cleveland Circular. It developed in the 12th-century, along with the construction of the stone castle and the nearby Rievaulx Abbey. In its early days it was an important centre for weaving woollen products, a fact reflected in the naming of the 'Dyers' bridge' next to the old Town Hall. Much of the older part of the town dates from the 17th-century, when the weaving trade was at its height. In more recent times it has become an important tourist centre, with its historic buildings surrounding the impressive market cross and the gothic-style memorial to the second Lord Feversham.

The town is home to several good pubs and hotels, some of them former coaching inns, such as the Black Swan Hotel. William Wordsworth and his sister Dorothy stayed at the Manor House on Castlegate in 1802, on their way to visit William's fiancée at Hackness. There are also numerous cafés just off the market square, and on the road leading south, which runs next to a small brook now enclosed by low stone walls.

At the south of the town are the impressive ruins of Helmsley Castle, now under the control of English Heritage. The castle was constructed in the 1120s by Sir Walter Espec, probably to replace an earlier motte and bailey castle. The castle was further extended in the 14th-century, with the construction of an eastern tower. Finally, in the 16th-century, the castle was substantially altered to create more spacious living apartments, using the wealth generated by the acquisition of Rievaulx Abbey by the Manners family, who now owned the castle.

By the 18th-century the castle had finally been abandoned for the much more agreeable living arrangements at the nearby Duncombe Park. The house was built in 1713-18 by Thomas Duncombe to a design of William Wakefield, a local architect. In 1845 it was enlarged according to the design of Sir John Barry, the architect famous for his reconstruction of the Houses of Parliament. The house was severely damaged by fire in the late 19th-century and was leased out to a preparatory school for girls. Only in 1986 did the house come back into the possession of the Faversham family. Unfortunately the house is now closed to visitors except for special events, but the delightful grounds are still open.

Next to the castle is Helmsley Walled Garden, an 18th-century garden built originally to supply flowers for the Feversham family. It fell into disuse during the First World War, but has now been restored to its former glory. The gardens cover five acres of land and provide a very

Market Square at Helmsley

tranquil place to relax after a long ride, with the opportunity to obtain much-needed refreshments.

The weary cyclist, if he or she has the energy, should try and get to see Helmsley castle or the walled garden, as they are both fascinating places. Alternatively, you might just want to unwind by walking through the little winding streets of this charming village.

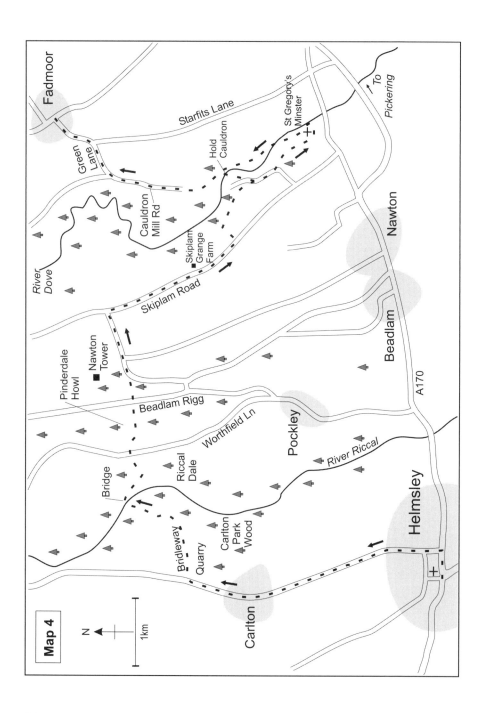

Map 4

34

2: In and Out of the Southern Dales

Day 2	Helmsley to Pickering (Maps 4-6)
Distance	25 miles
Allow	5 hours
Terrain	Initially a series of hills and ridges with some steep climbs and difficult paths. Most of this part is on bridleways across fields and through woods. Later on, the route follows the tarmac road and is more undulating with only two uphill sections of note
Toilets	Helmsley, Gillamoor, Hutton-le-Hole and Pickering
Refreshments	Pubs at Gillamoor, Lastingham and Cropton; pubs and cafés at Hutton-le-Hole and Pickering

The secret valleys of the North York Moors

The second section of the route is more difficult to plan. This is because the southern end of the North York Moors is intersected by a number of valleys or dales, flowing north-south with few routes running west to east. This tends to split up the route, and requires the cyclist to ride up and down the various ridges and use some of these north-south routes. The most direct road to Pickering is of course along the A170, but that is not the kind of road this route is designed to follow. If you want to stay in the hills, you have to weave in and out of a series of valleys, until you reach a section of tarmac road beyond Sleightholme Dale, where there is an east-west road connecting Gillamoor to Cropton. Up to this point most of the route is on various bridleways and minor roads, often following in the footsteps of the Tabular Way, a walk which connects Helmsley and Scarborough. However, the scenery is quite often enchanting, as you enter the deep wooded valleys of Riccal Dale and Kirk Dale, places rarely explored by tourists.

You begin this section by taking the road from Helmsley to Carlton (see Map 4). This road can be reached by going a few yards along the A170 eastwards out of Helmsley or, if you wish to avoid the main road, it can also be reached via Canonsgarth Road, which is the back road, and runs just north of the parish church. Follow this road to its junction with Baxtons Road and turn right. This road leads to the Carlton Road at which junction you turn left to head uphill.

The Carlton road runs along the top of the ridge between Ash Dale and Riccal Dale, and it climbs slowly but continuously for nearly two miles up to the small village of Carlton. This is a bit of a slow start, and the road seems to drag on interminably at first, but your spirits rise as you see the banks of trees appearing on your right, which mark the boundary of Riccal Dale Woods.

About ½ mile beyond the village there is a bridleway off to the right (613 876) which is indicated 'Beadlam Rigg'. Turn here, and then take the left-hand path which runs along the edge of Carlton Park Wood before plunging into the wood itself, when the tree-line turns sharply left. The route then goes deeper into the wood before coming to a signpost, which indicates a turn-off to the right along the route for the Tabular Way. The path here is supposed to be a bridleway, but it is a very steep descent as it plunges into Riccal Dale, a situation made worse by the unstable soil. The path becomes steeper as you descend, with a sharp bank on the right lined with trees. The more adventurous cyclists will no doubt try to ride down here, but I found it easier to dismount and scramble down on foot. However, even walking with the bike is very tricky here due to the steepness of the track and the erosion of the surface. Sometimes I found it useful to grab onto the trees which lined the route to stop myself slipping down the hill. As cycle routes go this is definitely rather challenging – I really do not know how the horse-riders cope!

Eventually the path comes out at a forest road, which you cross and pick up the bridleway at the other side. A short and less steep section brings you to a gate on the left, which you go through, and then you follow the path parallel to the stream for a short distance, until coming to a bridge over which you can push your bike. The path on the other side runs over a farmer's field, which is rather steep, and this time going upwards; again it was easier to push rather than to ride up this section. The path goes to the left of Hasty Bank Farm and leads to a waymarked gate at the top of the field.

At this point, take the path to the left, which quickly turns sharp right and leads up the side of the bank. The route here is very steep and uneven, and again you might find it easier to walk this section. However, I did find the views over the valley quite impressive, especially early in the morning, with the mist just rising from the valley above the lines of conifer trees on the hillside. It was almost as if you were walking in an alpine valley somewhere in Switzerland.

Eventually you come out at the top of the bank, where you go through a gate leading to a field that is crossed by way of a bridleway. This soon brings you to a tarmac road called Northfield Lane (638 882), which we cross over to pick up the bridleway at the other side. Over the road, the bridleway continues into another field, where we skirt around the right-hand edge until arriving at a waymarked gate. This leads us into a short section of wood known as Pinderdale Howl. The track runs along the side of the field, then turns off to the right down into a little wooded valley. Although this is a pleasant ride in normal circumstances, it can be very muddy and difficult to cycle through after wet weather. The path eventually climbs out of the other side of the beck along a short track.

Coming out of the wood, you cycle over another field before crossing a tarmac road (Beadlam Rigg). Again, there is a bridleway sign opposite (also indicating the Tabular Way), which leads across another field and then into a brief section of wood at the far right-hand corner of the field. Go through the waymarked gate into the woods, and you quickly come out onto another tarmac road by the entrance to Nawton Hall. Here you turn left towards the entrance, and quickly follow the road off to the right, which runs to the south of the hall. You can get a view of the building on your left from the road as you cycle by, once you go beyond the trees. This road provides a good stretch of easy riding for about ½ mile, where you can get a good burst of speed and admire the panoramic views – so long as you don't go too fast! After feeling a bit hemmed in whilst going through a series of valleys, fields and woods, I felt that this part of the route was quite liberating, and gave me a chance to feel the wind in my hair at last!

This road finally meets the Skiplam Road, a road running north-south along an open ridge. Turn south down the Skiplam Road and cycle about 1½ miles until you see a bridleway indicated on the left (660 867). This is about ½ mile beyond Skiplam Grange Farm, and is indicated as a bridleway, with a sign which refers to Hold Caldron. The bridleway runs along the left side of a field, at the end of which is a wooden gate which you go through and turn right. The bridleway then skirts the side of a wooded slope, and although the path here is grassed over, the route is downhill and cycling is easy, if a bit bumpy. After an exciting few minutes of downhill cycling, the route turns sharp left to lead onto an even steeper and ultimately rockier track, which ends at the weir by Hold Caldron. If you do cycle all the way down, you need to watch yourself at the end, as the track is very uneven with some sharp drops.

Hold Caldron is a collection of farm buildings, nestling in the bottom of the beautiful valley of Kirk Dale. Here the sides of the valley rise steeply, clothed in woodlands, creating a very peaceful, almost magical setting. Moreover, if you make only a slight diversion you will come to the picturesque Saxon church of St. Gregory's Minster, which lies about a mile to the south (677 858).

To get to the minster, turn off sharply to the right before the bridge over the river, and head down the road by the side of the valley. The road takes you into a secluded gorge with limestone walls. By the roadside you will find the remains of a limestone kiln used in the early industrial era. The road then turns sharply to the right, but you

Hold Caldron

St. Gregory's Minster

should carry on straight ahead along a bridleway through the woods, and soon you will see the minster down below on the left. The valley widens as you go south to create a amphitheatre, surrounded by limestone cliffs. The stream in the gorge has a mysterious habit of disappearing into its bed when the water level is low, because it then runs through a series of subterranean channels.

There is an alternative route back to Hold Caldron along a bridleway behind the church, but you need to cross the river by a ford which may be difficult at times of high water levels.

The minster was probably built in the 7th-century as an outpost of the monastery at Lastingham. Whilst parts of the original Anglo-Saxon church remain, the tower, despite its appearance, is actually a 19th-

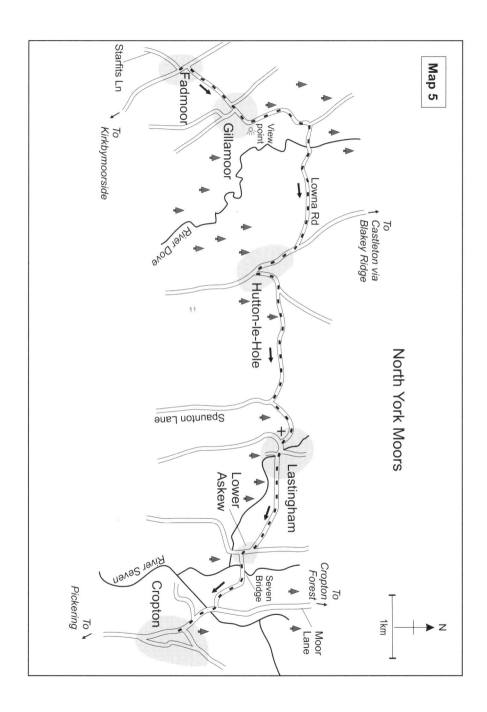

Map 5

North York Moors

Fadmoor

Gillamoor

Viewpoint

River Dove

Starfits Ln

To Kirkbymoorside

Lowna Rd

To Castleton via Blakey Ridge

Hutton-le-Hole

Spaunton Lane

Lastingham

Lower Askew

Cropton

River Seven

Seven Bridge

Cropton Forest

To Cropton Forest

Moor Lane

To Pickering

N

1km

41

century addition. The most interesting feature is the Anglo-Saxon sundial, just above the southern doorway. It dates from the mid-11th-century, and commemorates the rebuilding of the church in the decade before the Norman conquest.

To continue the main route from Hold Caldron, cross over the river and then turn left up a gentle slope, which follows the route of the Tabular Hills Link, as indicated by the appropriate signs. This path later turns uphill to the right and goes through another gate, before eventually bringing you out of the woods onto Caldron Mill Road. This is really a muddy track, but at least is easier to pedal along and is on the level. Gradually the aspect becomes more open and you look across a series of cultivated fields. Finally, this track leads to Green Lane, a small tarmac road, at which you turn right. You have come to the end of the off-road section on this part of the route and there are no more muddy paths to negotiate. Whilst this might seem a bit of a relief at the time, I rather regretted the end of this varied and sometimes quite atmospheric part of the trail.

A tale of two villages

The going now becomes much easier with tarmac roads and open moorland for most of the time. Green Lane soon runs into Starfitts Lane, at which you turn left. Continue up Starfitts Lane (see Map 5), and soon you will join the minor road which runs through Fadmoor and then onto Gillamoor. Although the pub at Fadmoor is currently closed, the Royal Oak pub at Gillamoor serves food and is open most days at lunchtime. Alternatively, you can go on another two miles to Hutton-le-Hole, to get a wider range of refreshments.

The two villages of Fadmoor and Gillamoor lie only about half a mile from each other on the top of the Tabular Hills. They are both moorland villages, built on limestone, close to the escarpments at the northern tip of the hills.

Fadmoor is the smaller of the two settlements and lies at the end of Rudland Rigg, the old drovers' track, which runs all the way from Blowarth crossing and was an important route in medieval times. The village is built around a small village green and was once very important for its local sheep market.

The village is the birthplace of Joseph Foord, well known as a 'hydraulic engineer'. He was able to devise a series of water races which brought water to the moorland villages of Fadmoor and Gillamoor from the moorland springs to the north. This system was later to be extended to several other settlements in the area including Carlton, Old Bylands and Rievaulx, all of which we pass through, or near, on the cycle route. The evidence of this engineering achievement can best be viewed from the car park at the top of Newgate Bank where it is just possible to see the grooves of the water-races cut into the nearby moorland hills.

The village of Gillamoor is slightly larger and has both a church and a pub. The pub is called 'The Royal Oak' and it serves real ale and bar meals. I found this a convenient place to stop after the off-road section. The church is called St. Aidan's, and it stands at the eastern edge of the village, where the road to Hutton turns sharply to the left. At this point the land falls away sharply and it is possible to get a magnificent view of the Farndale valley, a view referred to as 'Surprise View', as it is quite unexpected. The church was built in 1802 by James Smith of Farndale, and is notable for having no windows on its northern and eastern walls, no doubt to keep out the bitter winds in winter. Finally, you might note the remarkable four-faced sundial in the centre of the village, which was erected in 1800 by a Mr John Russell and is now a listed monument. This is on the left-hand side of the road as you cycle through the village, and is set back a little from the road.

At the far end of Gillamoor, just past the church, the road runs sharply down a slope towards the River Dove. You continue down

the road, avoiding the left-hand turn, and continue over the Lowna Bridge that crosses the river. The going here is very easy and no pedalling is required! However, this is only a short break, for then you have to cycle up Hutton Knowl, which was for me a hard slog on a hot day in the baking sun. Once the high ground is reached, you come quickly to the junction with the Blakey Road, which runs along Blakey Ridge from Castelton to Hutton-le-Hole. Turn right at the junction and the road then runs downhill quickly. Once again you can let gravity do the work, and very soon you can see the welcoming sight of Hutton-le-Hole before you (704 902).

An industrial village and a Saxon crypt

Hutton-le-Hole is a popular village with tourists and is well worth spending a little time to explore. There is a pub called 'The Crown' where you can sit out in the sunshine when the weather is good, and admire the view whilst drinking a pint. There are also tea-rooms on the main road where you can sit outside, such as the Forge Tea Rooms and The Barn Tea Rooms. Although this is well over halfway through this section, it is the first really obvious place to stop.

Hutton-le-Hole is a pretty little village which sprawls on either side of Hutton Beck, a shallow stream which runs through the common land in the middle of the village. The houses on the west of the beck are set back from the road, allowing for a large area of green common land through which the beck flows. Although this is now seen as a very attractive feature, the village was seen as ill-planned and disorganised by the Victorians.

Like so many villages in the North York Moors, its present rural charm belies its industrial past. In the 17th-century the village was developed by Quaker families and was known for its woollen and linen products. There is an old Quaker Meeting house in the centre of the village. However, in the 19th-century the village was the centre of ironstone mining, and housed a large population of miners. Conditions then

The Hutton Beck at Hutton-Le-Hole

were much worse than today, with no piped water and very little in the way of sanitation. The miners were often the worse for drink, and the green was populated by farm animals such as sheep, donkeys, geese and ducks – as well as drunken miners! The village then was not a particularly attractive place to visit!

How all that has changed! The village is now a key tourist centre and is the site of the Rydedale Folk Museum. If you have the time to visit the museum, you will see how the people of the area lived in previous centuries. Maybe then you will see how the present-day beauty of the village is really only a modern phenomenon.

You then take the road to Lastingham, which starts by heading north out of Hutton, before quickly turning eastwards and

continuing for about 1½ miles to reach the village of Lastingham (730 905). The route here is easy to follow and runs with the moorland on the left-hand side, and farm settlements to the right. You ignore the turn-off to the right indicated to Spaunton, and instead bear slightly to the left and carry on eastwards. After another ½ mile, you descend swiftly into the little village of Lastingham with its imposing church on the right-hand side of the road. This stretch of the ride is generally downhill, and I found that the distances here seemed to be covered very rapidly, so that I came upon the village with unexpected speed.

The village of Lastingham was the location for one of the earliest monasteries in England. In 654 AD St. Cedd, Bishop of the East Saxons, founded the monastery on behalf of King Ethelwald, the ruler of the Saxon kingdom of Diera, which stretched from Teesside to the Humber. This early monastery was probably built of wood, not stone, and so nothing now remains of it. St. Cedd was a key participant at the Synod of Whitby in 664 AD, which decided that the English church would follow the Roman rites and not those of the Celtic church. He died shortly afterwards at Lastingham, of the plague, and was buried at the monastery. However, before 732 AD, a stone church had been erected in Lastingham at the site of the monastery, and his body was transferred to this church, which provided a more permanent home.

The Saxon monastery disappeared from the records in the 9th or 10th-century and it was probably destroyed by Danish raiders. All we know for certain is that in 1078 a new monastery was built, with its present-day church. However, the new monastery was not a success and seems to have been abandoned within a few years, but the church remained, becoming a parish church in 1228. At one time it was one of the most important churches in the North York Moors, but now serves a much smaller congregation. The church itself is an excellent example of a Norman church, complete with its own crypt. The crypt is adorned with Norman arches and has a very peaceful atmosphere. If you have the time, I would recommend a visit to the church, and especially the crypt, as you will find it quite a fascinating place.

Virtually opposite the church is the village pub called the 'Blacksmith's Arms'. This is a useful place to stop and have a well-earned drink in the beer garden. At one time, the local curate, Reverend Jeremiah Carter, was a regular performer at the pub, playing the fiddle on Sunday afternoons. This did not go down well with the ecclesiastical authorities, but Jeremiah argued successfully that providing entertainment in the afternoon ensured that local people actually attended the church services in the morning, so his musical activities were tolerated. Just around the corner from the Blacksmith's Arms you can see one of the springs dedicated to St. Cedd. There are

Sheep grazing on the green at Hutton-Le-Hole

several other holy wells in the surrounding area dedicated to St. Chad and St. Ovin as well as St. Mary Magdalene.

After passing through Lastingham, you turn eastwards out of the village along Ings Lane, toward the village of Cropton. You will soon need to start using the Outdoor Leisure Map Eastern Area (Explorer OL 27), this being an indication that you are starting to make some progress at last towards the east coast. The route follows the small road through the hamlet of Lower Askew and over Seven Bridge, before meeting the 'B' road which leads to Cropton. The going here is quite easy, the land being relatively low-lying as it runs into the flat-bottomed valley of the River Seven. However, as you progress along, the wooded heights of Cropton Forest come into view, whilst the ridge on which the village of Cropton stands can now be easily seen looming up ahead. A hill climb beckons the weary cyclist!

You turn right at the junction with the 'B' road and head up the steep hill which leads to the top of the ridge. After a hard time pedalling (or pushing the bike), you finally reach a sign for Cropton. Just at the entrance to the village is a bench on a grassy mound where the exhausted cyclist can rest. This was an offer I could not refuse, and I found that it was a very calming place to unwind, and to have a quick drink of water whilst taking in the scenery. After this, you turn sharp left and take the small road which runs right through the village, heading north and then east to Cropton Forest (see Map 6).

Medieval castles and a Roman camp

The village of Cropton lies at the south-western end of Cropton Forest, on high ground overlooking Cropton Beck, indeed the name probably means 'hill-top farm'. The village lies either side of the road which runs north and then east to Newton-on-Rawcliffe. There is a pub called the New Inn, which has had its own brewery since 1984. The pub also serves meals and can provide accommodation if required. To reach it,

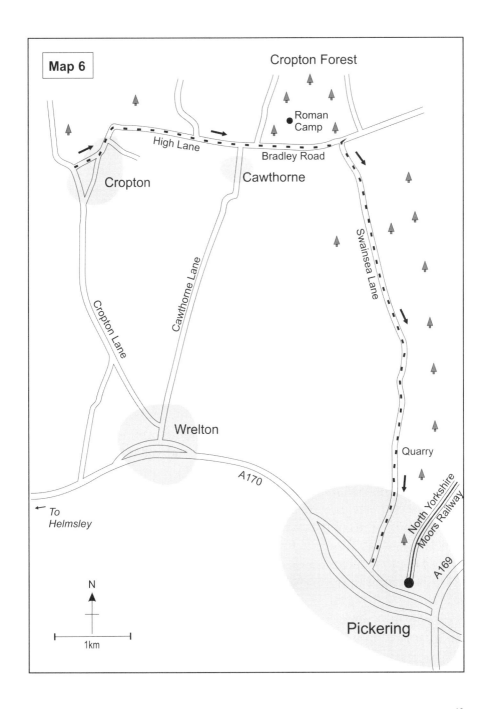

Map 6

Cropton Forest

Roman Camp

High Lane

Bradley Road

Cropton

Cawthorne

Swainsea Lane

Cropton Lane

Cawthorne Lane

Wrelton

A170

Quarry

To Helmsley

North Yorkshire Moors Railway

A169

Pickering

N

1km

continue south at the entrance to the village and it is just a few yards down the B road, which continues to Pickering.

This is a very picturesque village, with quaint rural cottages lining the main street and colourful gardens in front of them. On the right-hand side of the road, you might note a cottage with the inscription '1695 *memento mori* NC'. Just opposite, there is a small lane which leads off to the parish church of St. Gregory's. In the graveyard of the church is the stump of an ancient cross. There is a little ditty associated with this cross, which refers to the leaving of a cup of water there for a weary traveller to drink. It reads:

> *'On Cropton Cross there is a cup,*
> *And in that cup there is a sup,*
> *Take that cup and drink that sup,*
> *And set that cup on Cropton Cross Top'.*

To the right of the church is a small lane, which leads to the remains of a motte and bailey castle on the land behind the church. The castle is 12th-century and was constructed in wood by a Robert de Stuleville. It was never rebuilt in stone, and eventually fell into disuse, now being simply referred to as 'round hill'. The mound is well worth a visit, as it offers a marvellous view over the moors and valleys to the west.

Cropton is the birthplace of Captain William Scoresby, a famous Arctic explorer and whaler, who was the inventor of the 'crow's nest'. There is a monument to him at Whitby, where he was based for most of his life. His son was also called William, and he too was a famous captain, whose exploits included rounding up the Danish fleet after the battle of Copenhagen in the Napoleonic Wars.

You continue along the road out of the village to the north, which soon turns right to run along the south side of Cropton Forest, where it is called High Lane. The road here is quite undulating and

runs in a slight curve due east, with trees on both sides. In the late afternoon sun, I found that the trees on the right were a great boon, helping to keep me cool and keeping the sun out of my eyes. Suddenly you come across signs indicating a Roman Camp, this being the Roman Camp at Cawthorne (785 895) which you may wish to visit, if you are not in a desperate rush to get to Pickering.

The Roman camp lies about two miles to the north-east of Cropton, on the road to Newton-on-Rawcliffe. The site consists of four constructions dating from the late 1st to the early 2nd-century. These are now believed to consist of two forts, as well as a 'coffin-shaped' marching camp. This complex of fortifications lay on the route of the Roman road that connected Malton (*Derventio*) to Whitby (*Dictuim*). The road went via Lease Rigg, just outside Grosmont, and indeed part of the road is still visible on Wheeldale moor, just to the north of Cropton Forest. Before the planting of the Cropton Forest, the camp would have had extensive views over the Vale of Pickering, and so provided an excellent vantage point to control the area. It appears that the camp was abandoned some time after 120 AD, but there is evidence that it was used again in early medieval times, probably by Danish settlers. In addition, the medieval packhorse route known as the 'Porter Gate' also runs through the middle of the site, cutting through the marching camp.

About ½ mile past the entrance to the Roman Camp, you turn right off this road onto another road, signposted to Pickering. This is called Swainsea Lane, and, for the most part, it is possible to freewheel downhill for about three miles, right into the centre of Pickering. However, at first the road is undulating, and it is only after you reach the summit of the final hill next to the Queen's Plantation (793 883) that you can eventually see all the way down into the Vale of Pickering below. At this point, you seem to burst out of a veil of trees and start to race down to the lowlands below. Within a short time, you have reached the suburbs of Pickering, and very soon after, you come to a T-junction with a busy road. Turn left onto this road, and follow the hill down into the centre of the town, where you might be able to hear the whistle of the trains at the North Yorkshire Moors Railway, welcoming you to Pickering.

A town of many surprises

The station at Pickering is our final destination, and can be seen indicated off to the left about ¼ mile after the junction. This is a chance for a refreshing cup of tea, while you watch the hive of activity on the station platform, with the tourist trains coming from Grosmont. Later on in the trip you will pass the Grosmont end of the line, where there are some shunting-lines and engine sheds with a variety of rolling stock. For now, you are in Pickering where there are many things to do and visit.

Pickering is a small market town which lies on the south side of the North York Moors. By legend, it is said to have very early origins in Celtic times, but Pickering was really founded in the Saxon era as a market town. By the medieval period Pickering was a busy market centre, with various roads called 'gates' leading to the market place, such as Hungate, Birdgate and Borrowgate. In the 17th-century the town became famous for its non-conformist religious beliefs, being visited by George Fox the Quaker and the Methodist John Wesley. Pickering boomed until the 1960s, when the closure of the rail connection to Whitby led to a temporary decline. However, the rise of the tourist trade has much improved the fortunes of Pickering in recent times. There are many places to stay, as well as numerous pubs and cafés. Of particular note is the Beck Isle Museum of Rural Life which is well worth a visit.

The North Yorkshire Moors Railway starts from here, and the station has been recently refurbished with a new carriage shed. The station was originally built in 1845 and is constructed of sandstone. It has been fitted out in 1930s fashion by the North Yorkshire Moors Railway, and there are many items of platform furniture and fittings taken from other stations in the region. Of particular note is the turntable next to the carriage shed, which allows locomotives to be quickly turned around to face the correct direction of travel.

Apart from the railway station, there are many other interesting features in Pickering. The most prominent is the medieval castle which overlooks the railway from a steep cliff to the east of the town. It was erected in the late 11th-century as a motte and bailey construction. Henry II added a stone circular shell keep in the late 12th-century, after which the castle was rebuilt in stone. It has a chantry chapel built in 1227 and an old hall. It was used variously as a royal holiday home, a stud farm and a hunting lodge, but it gradually fell into disrepair in the 17th-century. At the other side of the town are the remains of a second castle which is much less complete. This was a motte and bailey castle, erected probably in the mid 12th-century during the civil wars in the reign of King Stephen. It was never rebuilt in stone and remains simply as a rampart known as 'beacon hill'. It was later used as an observation post by the Royal Observation Corps.

The parish church of Saints Peter and Paul is located at the east side of the market place and is certainly worth a detour. The church is of Saxon origin, but the existing construction is medieval. The most remarkable features are the medieval wall paintings which adorn most of the internal walls, and are a rarity in Britain. They were whitewashed over at the time of the Reformation, but later uncovered in the 19th-century. The paintings show a variety of scenes, including the Martyrdom of St. John the Baptist, St. George slaying the Dragon and the Passion of Christ. Despite the many years since they were completed, the paintings are still striking in appearance, and very evocative of the medieval world view of society, with the characters painted in contemporary costume.

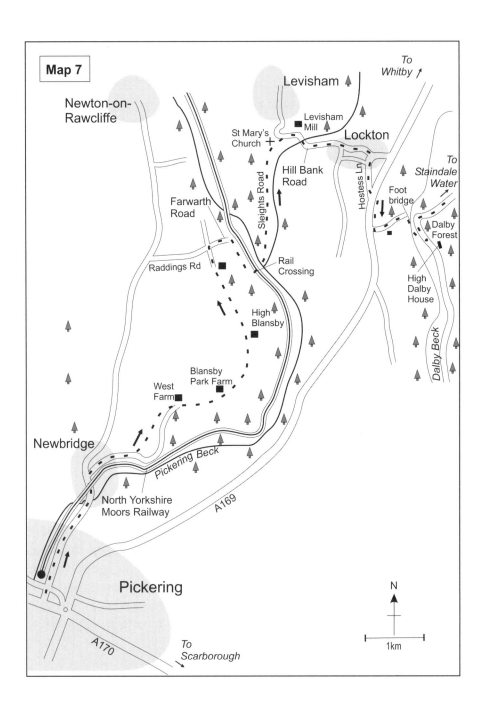

Map 7

Newton-on-Rawcliffe

Levisham

To Whitby

Levisham Mill

St Mary's Church

Lockton

Hill Bank Road

Hostess Ln

To Staindale Water

Farwarth Road

Sleights Road

Foot bridge

Dalby Forest

Raddings Rd

Rail Crossing

High Dalby House

High Blansby

Dalby Beck

Blansby Park Farm

West Farm

Newbridge

Pickering Beck

North Yorkshire Moors Railway

A169

Pickering

N

1km

A170

To Scarborough

3: Flying down to the sea

Day 3	Pickering to Scarborough (Maps 7-9)
Distance	23 miles
Allow	4½ hours
Terrain	Initial stage is hard going with some rough terrain, although not steep. The later section is on tarmac roads and is usually level with some long descents
Toilets	Pickering, Stain Dale, Dalby Visitor Centre, Scarborough
Refreshments	All the above (except Stain Dale) as well as a pub at Levisham (just off route) and Langdale End

Over the fields to Newton Dale

This is a varied section of the Cleveland Circular with a mixture of on-road and off-road cycling, with most of the off-road cycling at the beginning. The final section involves a long downhill section on a tarmac road, which is very exhilarating and also a welcome relief after a lot of hard cycling. At first the progress is slow, but the final section is completed quickly, so that the whole journey can be completed in 4 to 5 hours with a brief stop.

You start the third leg of the circular from the railway station at Pickering and head up the main road to Newton-on-Rawcliffe (see Map 7). Although the railway line initially runs on your left-hand side, you soon cross over the line at a level crossing, at the inappropriately named Newbridge. Just after crossing the line, there is a track off to the right called Bransby Park Lane, which you follow for a short distance past farm buildings at Park Gate. Just beyond, is a sign stating 'Private Road', before you come across the entrance to a bridleway on the left, leading into a small wood. The track is steep here and a little too slippery to cycle up, so you might find it easier to push the bike here.

At the top, after going through a gate, the route runs across a small field and then joins a clearly-marked farm track, at which you turn left and cycle to the south of West Farm. The view opens up well at this point and you can see the woods on the top of Pickering Beck to your right, through which the railway runs. You then go through a gate and continue on an obvious farm track, with blue bridleway markings on the gates and occasional posts. This follows round Blansby Park Farm (827 867), after which it degenerates into a rutted track crossing several fields; at this point it is possible to see the outline of some woods ahead.

Eventually, you come to a gate at a gap in a hedgerow, after which you pass High Blansby Farm, which is now a derelict farm building. The entrance to the woods is now clearly seen ahead, with the track disappearing into its hidden depths. Once in the woods, I found the track to be very rutted with frequent boggy patches which made it hard-going at times. However, enclosed by the trees, it felt very peaceful and atmospheric, and almost seemed to spirit you away to another world of endless forests – like something out of Tolkien. Although it was only a short stretch of the route, I rather enjoyed this brief run through the woods.

Finally, you emerge from the path through the woods onto a rocky track, which leads down to Ruddings Road, a minor road running east from the Newton Road which you left about 30 minutes before. The way is downhill and rough-going, leading you through a farmyard and a couple of gates, before reaching the road. At this point, you turn right down Ruddings Road, and almost immediately you come to Farwarth Road, which is really a steep track off to the right, leading down to the railway. This is difficult to cycle because of the loose surface, and I found it easier to walk the last bit down to the railway.

At the bottom, you cross a ford, and then immediately cross the railway line at a level-crossing at Farwath (828 884). On the other side of the railway you continue straight ahead (do not go left over the stream), until you reach a gate with a bridleway sign. Immediately after going through the gate, you turn sharp left up a slope, and come quickly to a second waymarked gate which leads onto the Sleights Road.

By the side of Levisham Beck

Sleights Road is a sandy, undulating track which runs through the woods at the side of a stream for about a mile, to eventually join a tarmac road. The sides of the track can be slippery, and there is rather a long drop to the stream below, so I suggest careful cycling at this point! You begin with a gradual climb through the woods before the path eventually levels out. This leads to a high-level pathway through an avenue of trees, with a dramatic view of the deepening valley to your left. At this point, you may hear the distant sounds of the trains on the North Yorkshire Moors Railway, down in Newton Dale, reminding you of where you have just come from. Very soon, you will notice a red-roofed house on the hills opposite, nestling in the slopes of Rowl Wood. A few minutes later and you come to another gate, at which point it is possible to see the tower of St. Mary's church in the valley below.

Just after the gate, there is a track off to the left-hand side, which runs down to the valley bottom and crosses the stream by way of a wooden bridge. This is actually the route of the bridleway, but there is no indication as such at the turn, and it is easy to miss. When you follow this path, you will soon come to the deserted church of St. Mary's at the bottom of the valley.

The parish church of St. Mary's dates from the 12th-century, although it was substantially rebuilt in 1802. The church is no longer used today, and now stands roofless, exposed to the elements, a very poignant sight. This is a quiet spot, which offers a great opportunity to enjoy a few minutes of quiet contemplation before returning to the route.

After passing the church, you follow the track up a gravelly slope on the other side, to join Mill Bank Road, which runs from Levisham down to Lockton via Levisham mill. Turn right to go down the hill and you will come to Levisham Beck with the mill on your left-hand side.

St. Mary's Church at Levisham

Levisham Mill

On the beck itself is Levisham Mill, a water-mill first referred to in 1246. It was refurbished in the 19th-century and was later provided with a cast-iron water-wheel. However, the mill stopped production in 1963 and it is now in a poor state of repair. The location of the mill is truly idyllic, in the bottom of a steeply-wooded valley, which is now packed full of wildlife including the occasional deer.

At the other side of the beck the road rises steeply and I found it a bit of a pull to get to the top. However, after about ¼ mile from the beck, the road turns sharp right and you come suddenly into the village of Lockton. The road comes to a junction at which you should go straight ahead.

Lockton and Levisham are two villages which lie on either side of Levisham Beck. The cycle route takes us through Lockton, which is the larger of the two villages, and is of Anglo-Saxon origin with a small church and village green. However, it is worth a short detour to visit Levisham, which can be reached by turning left at the end of the bridleway, and going up Mill Bank Road to the village, which lies up the slope on high ground at the north side of the beck.

Although Levisham is at the top of a hill, it is connected by a steep road to Levisham Station on the North Yorkshire Moors railway in the valley of Newton Dale. The original settlement was located near St. Mary's Church in the valley below, but the inhabitants seemed to have vacated that site, possibly because it was affected by the Black Death. If this is the case, it is a similar story to the one we came across at Whorlton and Swainby, on the first leg of the journey. Levisham is a one-road village lined by some lovely houses, with a pub at the end called the Horshoe Inn, should you wish to have a drink.

Into Dalby Forest

The route now continues a short distance beyond the junction, before you come to a fork in the road. Take the sharp right-hand turn and this will quickly bring you to a minor road called Hostess Lane which runs to the A169. Turn right into this road and follow it down to the main road. Just before the end of Hostess Lane, you may notice on the right-hand side a cycle lane, which you can then take. At the A169, you cross the road and there is a continuation of this cycle route at the side of the main road. This runs on the left of the A169 for about ¼ mile before it runs into a minor road leading off the A169 (845 887).

The minor road runs down a steep hill, passing a sign indicating the 'Moor to Sea' Cycle Route. You soon pass a bungalow on the right before coming to a sign indicating Staindale Lodge off to the left. Just after this point the view opens up before you, revealing a scenic valley with Dalby Forest on your left. The road becomes a track, which then winds majestically off into the valley bottom. The bridleway is clearly marked, and the track soon turns off to the left. Cross a wooden bridge, and within a few yards you come to the Dalby Forest Drive next to High Dalby House.

Dalby Forest is part of the large area of forested land in the south-east of the North York Moors. Most of the forest is now open for leisure activities, such as walking and cycling, and there is a comprehensive set of mountain-bike routes which are all waymarked. The Dalby Forest Visitor Centre (856 874) is a short detour from the route, and here it is possible to obtain refreshments and information about the forest tracks. However, the circular route will be using the tarmac road which serves as the Dalby Forest Drive, so you will need to return north up this road and head towards Stain Dale.

Dalby Forest is home to a large number of birds and animals, including roe deer and the greater spotted woodpecker, although you might not see them as you race by on your bike! However, there is a small lake called Stain Dale Water where you can relax and wait for the wildlife to come to you.

The forest is a very well-used facility with picnickers, hikers and of course cyclists, not forgetting the 'hard core' mountain bikers who race through the woods seeking the most death-defying descents. You will usually find a lot going on, especially in the summer, so the woods will be a hive of activity – in fact it is sometimes like a miniature version of the Lake District at its busiest. However if you cycle on, you will always find somewhere less crowded in the forest, where you can relax with just the sounds of the forest for company.

The circular route uses the obvious Dalby Forest Drive, but you are always at liberty to use other routes through the woods, so long as you eventually reach the Bickley Gate exit. Indeed this may be necessary if the Forest Drive is closed, which happens occasionally. For example, there is a suggested route starting just north of the Visitor Centre (856 879), which can be followed up to Ingleby Tower (889 891). I leave this up to you.

When you enter Dalby Forest you need to turn left onto the Dalby Forest Drive, and head towards Stain Dale Water (880 903) (see Map 8). This is a pleasant place to have a packed lunch if you have brought one, with seats to sit on and a relaxing view over the small lake, surrounded by the forest. Having passed the north side of the lake, you go round a sharp bend and follow a slight slope along the south side of the lake towards Adderstone Wood. The scenery here is very relaxing, and when I completed the route I recall seeing

Stain Dale Water

glimpses of the lake sparkling in the sunlight as I cycled past. Once at the top of this slope, it turns sharply left, almost going back on itself, and then runs due south-east until, after ¾ mile, the road turns sharp left at Ingleby Tower (889 891). This is an area which is mainly tree-lined, but you may note that there are some large open areas set aside for picnicking.

The forest drive then runs north-east to Bickley Gate for about 1½ miles, with open fields eventually coming into view on your right-hand side. The road gradually bears to the right, before tumbling down a steep hill, and then turning sharp right to the Toll Booth at Bickley Gate. This section is all downhill and you will find yourself racing past the toll booth – fortunately there is no charge for bikes! A short stretch of road then brings you to a T-junction just beyond Blackwood Bungalow, where there is a red telephone box opposite (914 923).

Rollercoasting down the Langdale road

At this junction you will see a sign saying '10 miles to Scarborough'. After such hard work, it seems that you have only done just over half the route! However, do not despair, as the next part of the journey is really very easy, and you will find that the miles slip by quickly. Turn right at this point, and the road now starts to lead south-eastwards, downhill into Langdale, and finally to the village of Hackness. The scenery here is breathtaking, with forested hills on either side of this peaceful valley. The cycling is fantastic, with the farms and little settlements flying by as gravity whisks you down the long, sloping valley. It was almost as if you were on a roller coaster, rattling along at breakneck speed.

Just less than two miles beyond Bickley Gate, there is a pub called The Moorcock at Langdale End, which has a tea-room serving light snacks in the summer-time. This is a very pleasant place to halt, if you can bring yourself to stop the fun! There are

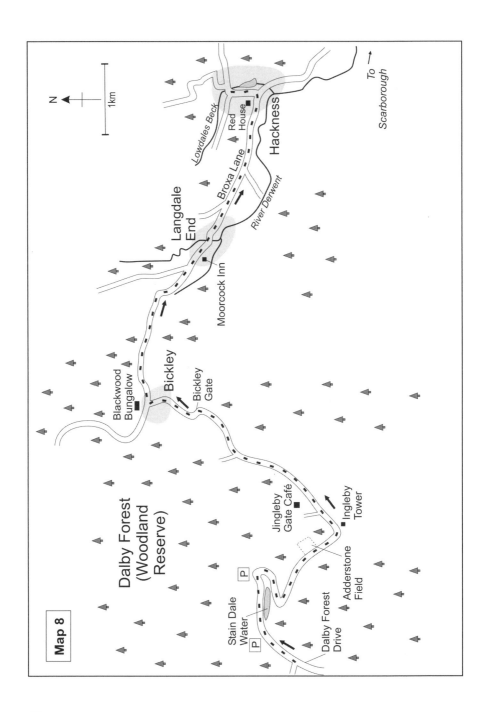

Map 8

Dalby Forest (Woodland Reserve)

Stain Dale Water

Dalby Forest Drive

Adderstone Field

Ingleby Tower

Jingleby Gate Café

Bickley

Bickley Gate

Blackwood Bungalow

Moorcock Inn

Langdale End

Broxa Lane

River Derwent

Lowdales Beck

Red House

Hackness

To → Scarborough

N

1km

seats on the adjoining grass verge, where I took the opportunity to bask in the afternoon sunshine, downing a welcome pint of beer, when I did the trip. If you haven't had a break yet, now is the time to take it!

Finally, the road drops down to a T-junction by the so-called Red House opposite the war memorial (968 901), and you take the left-hand road with the sign indicating Suffield and Scalby. This road leads you round the back of Hackness Hall and through the peaceful estate village of Hackness.

The estate village of Hackness is the location for Hackness Hall, the country home of the Derwent family, which dates from 1777. There is a small freshwater lake in front of the hall, which once provided fresh fish for the residents. The hall also has an ice house, hidden nearby in the trees, where food could be stored in ice to stay fresh, before the days of the refrigerator. There are some interesting water conduits and ornamental walls, and you get a good view of the Hall and the lake in its grounds from the approach road. Also of note are the outbuildings for the hall, located on the hill on your left-hand side as you round the back of the hall. The road at the rear of the hall has a stream running beside it, which mysteriously appears from the supports of the stone bridge crossing over the road. Maybe this is a spring which was used to provide water for people in the village.

Across the road, you might notice the Church of Saint Peter, originally founded in 680 AD. This church is an amalgam of Saxon, Norman and Gothic features, with an 8th-century preaching cross beside it. The village was originally the site of a religious settlement of nuns from Whitby, and another religious settlement was built by the Benedictines in the 11th-century. However, there is little trace of these today; only the church remains.

Bridge at Hackness

When you leave Hackness, you cycle up Cross Dales Hill, which is a tiring pull at this point in the ride, but you do begin to feel that the end of this stage must be quite soon. This is in fact the last big haul upwards, and brings you, after about a mile, to a place called Suffield Farm and then to Northfield Farm, the former name, possibly corrupted from Southfield over time (986 906). Just after the second farm we take the road off to the right called Hay Lane (later Hackness Road), which speeds us down to the village of Scalby.

At last – the sea!

The village of Scalby is really a suburb of Scarborough, divided from the town by Scalby Beck. This is fed by the North Back Drain or Sea Cut, a flood-relief channel which drains the water from the whole of the south-east of the moors. The village has an old centre with a 12th-century church, and you can visit it if you wish. However, the route now continues on to Scarborough itself.

When you get to Scalby, ignore the turn off to the left indicated Scalby, and instead continue on the main road. This leads off to the right and quickly crosses the North Back Drain, part of the Sea Cut, before bending round to the left, and finally meeting the Scalby Road next to the Rosette Public House.

The end of this stage is the car-park by the beach next to Scalby Mills, not far from the Sea Life Centre. To get there involves cycling another mile or so through suburban roads before coming out at the car-park, on Burniston Road, close to the coast. To begin with, turn right at the junction of Hackness Road and Scalby Road, and continue along Scalby Road until you reach Green Lane, about ½ mile further on, where there is a sign for the North Cliff Golf Club. Turn left down Green Lane, which eventually becomes Cross Lane and finally brings you out at Burniston Road. A right turn down Burniston Road soon brings you to the entrance to the car park on the left-hand side.

This is a fitting place to end this stage, conveniently close to many places for refreshments, as well as providing an opportunity to take in the sea air. From here you can easily get down to the front and cycle into the town along the Promenade. This is a fascinating ride in itself, past fishing boats, amusement arcades and around the castle, enabling you to explore the town of Scarborough at your leisure.

Scarborough lies at the end of the third stage of the cycle route and it is well worth spending some time here. The town itself is by far the largest on the route, and is indeed one of the most important holiday resorts in the UK. Moreoever, it is also a place with a fascinating history.

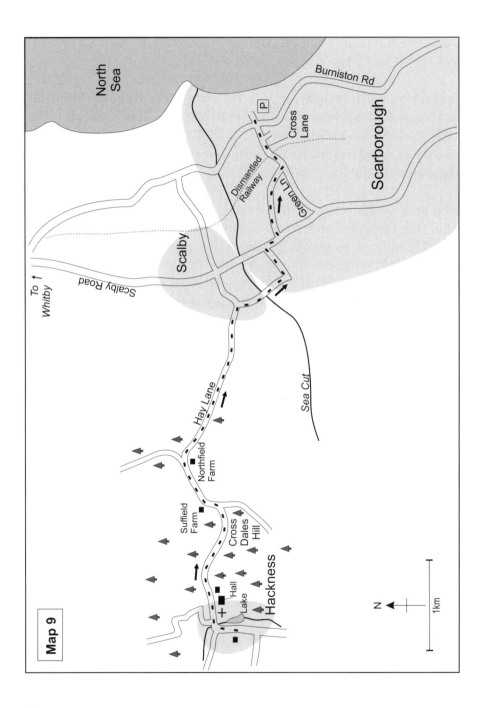

Map 9

North Sea

Burniston Rd

Scarborough

P

Cross Lane

Dismantled Railway

Green Ln

Scalby

Scalby Road

To Whitby

Sea Cut

Hay Lane

Northfield Farm

Suffield Farm

Cross Dales Hill

Hackness

Hall

Lake

N

1km

The town was founded in 966 AD by the Vikings, although there had been a Roman signal station on the headland since the 4th-century. The town really began to develop after the stone castle was erected there in the mid-11th-century by Henry II. The castle was provided with massive defensive walls, and yet it was captured with very little effort in 1554, by a group of rebels under the leadership of Sir Thomas Stafford. The town was also an important market town, with the famous 'Scarborough Fair' starting in 1233 and continuing for 500 years. The fair is of course commemorated by a famous folk song of the same name.

Scarborough's rise as a tourist resort began when a local spring was discovered in the 17th-century, which helped to develop the town as a spa resort. Its growth was further enhanced by the arrival of the railway in 1845, which made it much easier for people to get there. Scarborough's famous Grand Hotel was begun in 1867 and was constructed with 12 floors, 52 chimneys and (at one time) 365 rooms. The subsequent construction of the Spa complex, and the development of Peasholm Park, finally confirmed Scarborough as a major holiday resort.

Today the town has developed many more attractions, such as the Sea Life Centre and the recently revamped Open Air Theatre. Most of the children's attractions are in the North Bay to the north of the headland, whilst the South Bay caters more for older visitors. The town centre also has a wide variety of interesting pubs and cafés and if you have some extra time and energy at the end of your ride, you might want to give them a visit. Of course, it is also an easy place to find accommodation at most times of the year, if you are intending to stay overnight.

4: Smugglers' haunts and sunlit bays

Day 4	Scarborough to Whitby (Maps 10-12)
Distance	20 Miles
Allow	4 hours
Terrain	This is a very easy-going route, almost all along a disused railway line. There are slight inclines, but none of them should pose any problems
Toilets	Ravenscar, Robin Hood's Bay, Whitby
Refreshments	Pubs at Burniston, Hayburn Wyke, Robin Hood's Bay and Whitby, Cafés at Cloughton, Ravenscar, Robin Hood's Bay and Whitby

The land of forgotten railway stations

This stage of the Cleveland Circular is arguably one of the most scenic, and also the fastest. Most of the route follows the course of the disused railway line from Scarborough to Whitby, which is now a designated cycleway known as the 'Cinder Track'. The first half of the route is slightly uphill, but the delightful wooded scenery for much of the distance makes up for this, and the going is not too hard. Once you reach Ravenscar, the route starts to head downhill, just as you get your first glimpse of the sea. The downhill section is a real delight, with fast cycling and spectacular views over the cliff tops along the way. Right at the end of the railway line you turn off into Whitby, where there is plenty of accommodation for the night.

The 20-mile Scarborough-Whitby Railway opened in 1885, and at once provided easy access to places such as Robin Hood's Bay, which had previously been very difficult to reach. This helped to boost the tourist trade for these coastal towns at a time when car travel was not possible for most people, and indeed the grandiose development plans for Ravenscar were based on the presence of the railway.

The route itself was certainly very scenic, with its tunnels and cliff-top views, but it was never very profitable because it had cost so much to build. It did enjoy a brief boom period between the World Wars, when the holiday trade began to expand rapidly. However, the arrival of affordable motoring undermined the position of rail travel from the 1960s, and the line closed in 1965, a victim of the Beeching cuts.

The disused railway track begins in the suburbs of Scarborough and runs from Manor Road Cemetery (see Map 10). You need to pick it up a little to the north, where it passes under Cross Lane, the road you cycled down in the previous stage to get to the car park at Scalby Mills. The cycleway runs under a bridge on Cross Lane, and there is a short path leading from the main road next to a sign saying 'no vehicles', as well as a blue National Cycle Route sign.

The first section is an urban cycle-route, which runs through the suburban development at Newby. The route peters out at Chichester Close, and you need to cycle down the short close to Station Road, turn right, and then quickly left, into Field Close Road. You should notice a green sign on Station Road indicating the way to the 'trackway.' Go along Field Close Road for a few yards and take Lancaster Way, which branches off to the right. The start of the railway route is down a path on your right, just before the last bungalow at the end of this cul-de-sac (016 909).

After all this urban cycling, it is nice to get into the countryside again. The cycleway leads out into open fields, soon going in a straight line towards the village of Burniston, about a mile to the north. This first section is quite open to the elements, although sometimes the route becomes tree-lined, which provides a little

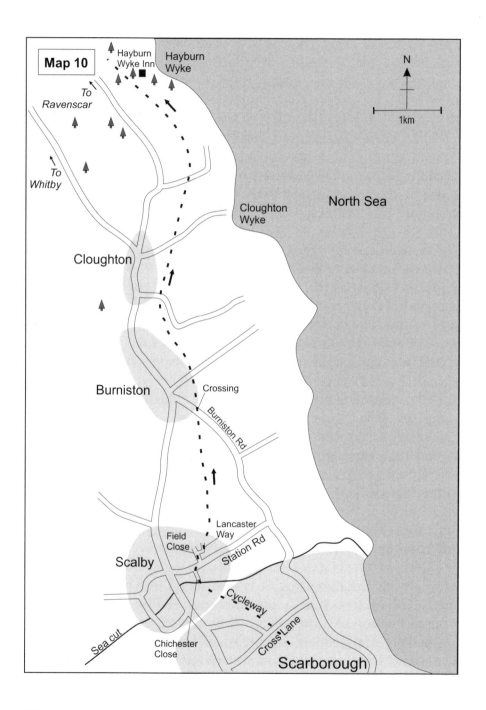

Map 10

Hayburn
Wyke Inn
Hayburn
Wyke

To
Ravenscar

To
Whitby

N

1km

North Sea

Cloughton
Wyke

Cloughton

Burniston

Crossing

Burniston Rd

Lancaster
Way

Field
Close

Station Rd

Scalby

Cycleway

Sea cut

Chichester
Close

Cross Lane

Scarborough

cover from the rain and wind. Otherwise, you can see over the fields to both sides, with the track heading towards the horizon. This was the point at which I felt that the real cycle ride had begun, with the rugged coast of North Yorkshire waiting ahead. Eventually the route leads you to a little wooden bridge, which turns at a right angle over a stream and brings you to the village of Burniston.

Burniston is a small village which was infamous in the 18th and 19th centuries for smuggling. There are two pubs which can be visited there as well as a café on the route itself which sells ice creams. However, as you have just started off on the journey you would not want to stop at this early stage – would you?

At Burniston, the cycleway crosses the A165 or the Burniston Road, and skirts the east of the village towards the coast. The route now meanders slightly to the west, before passing to the east of the village of Cloughton, where it passes in front of the disused village railway station. Part of this has now been converted into a café called the Station Tea Rooms, where it is possible to get refreshments between Saturday and Wednesday. After the station, you cross a road and the track continues on the other side, just a little to the right. The route then leads out of the village, crossing another minor road, which runs down to the scenic cove at Cloughton Wyke with its dramatic cliff face (020 950). If you have time, you may wish to make a detour to reach this down a tarmac road.

Shortly after this point, the cycleway veers to the east, running parallel to the coast and eventually starts to enter a partly-wooded area, which provides much-needed shade and shelter. The land between the track and the coast gradually begins to rise into a ridge, shutting you off from the sea. This provides some extra protection from the wind, so that this part of the route seems quite enclosed, in contrast to the open country we have just passed through. The going is quite good here, and the area appears to be quite uninhabited, until you suddenly come across the whitewashed walls and bright-red, tiled roof of Northend House, lying to the right of the track, seemingly in the middle of nowhere.

Just over ½ mile later you come across the Inn at Hayburn Wyke, which is set in the bottom of a tranquil, wooded vale adjoining the nature reserve of Hayburn Wyke (009 970). The inn serves food and drinks and there is a place to sit outside the pub in this sunny, sheltered spot. If you want a break at this stage, this is a place well worth spending some time. The route then starts to turn away from the coast, initially taking a big curve before straightening out (see Map 11). The going is quite easy here with woodland cover for most of the way, providing quite a pleasant cycling experience. Then, suddenly, you come out of the woods and arrive at the disused station at Bridge Farm. The change of scene is dramatic, and you feel that the station has just appeared out of a deep forest. The station is certainly impressive, with its long, imposing platform and extensive station buildings opposite. In addition, the location is quite open with views over to the sea, no longer obstructed by any hills. This is a good place to stop and take a picture – I certainly did!

The route then runs parallel to the coast with intermittent woodland cover, the sea views closed off again. The track starts to get a bit difficult at this point, with the surface quite uneven, possibly because of erosion by rainwater. Most of the route is gradually uphill as we cycle to the ford near Meeting House Farm about two miles further on. After this point, the track improves a little, but I still found it hard-going at times, always having to watch carefully where I was cycling so as to avoid the ruts.

Eventually the cycleway emerges from the woods, and starts to rise slightly as you turn east towards the coast. This is the last stretch

Re-used station on the Whitby Line at Bridge Farm

before you come to Ravenscar, and soon you are able to see the sea for nearly the first time since you left Scarborough. The route also leaves the southern half of the North York Moors (Eastern Area) OS map, an indication of progress northwards. The cycle track gradually approaches the coast, and the red roofs of the buildings at Ravenscar (980 014) come slowly into view. Eventually you arrive at the station platform, below which is the station square, with a row of houses on the north side.

The town that never was

You leave the cycleway just before the disused railway platform, and cycle into the square, which would have been the centrepiece of a major new holiday resort, had things turned out differently. There are refreshments available at the Ravenscar Tearooms at the far end of the terrace, directly in front of you, these being open every day from April to October. Alternatively, you can turn left by the tearooms and cycle the short distance along Station Road to the Raven Hall Hotel where it is also possible to get a meal in more sumptuous surroundings (but at a slightly more sumptuous price). I would recommend taking tea in the gardens as the view to the north is breathtaking – but do watch out if it gets windy!

Ravenscar is a small village perched on top of the massive cliffs of the Yorkshire coast, lying about half-way between Scarborough and Whitby. Yet this quiet little settlement has had a varied and often chequered history, which is revealed through the remains of the industrial activity which surrounds it.

The site was originally the location of a Roman signal station, one of the many stations along this coast, which were designed to warn of the coming of the Saxons in the declining years of the Roman Empire in Britain. The village itself has a Viking-sounding name, but until the late 19th-century it was referred to simply as Peak.

In the 16th-century, the area around Ravenscar became famous for the production of alum, a chemical used to fix the colours in woollen and other fibres. The process of obtaining alum was very complicated, and involved a number of different activities. The alum-bearing rocks were mined nearby and were then heated up in huge fires for many months, before being soaked in water to extract the aluminium sulphate solution. To this mixture was added roasted seaweed and stale urine in order to produce the crystals known as alum. The activity died out in the mid-19th-century following the development of synthetic dyes, which did not require fixing in the same way.

Raven Hall Hotel, the imposing building at the north end of the village, was originally called 'Peak House' and was owned at one time by Doctor Francis Willis, sometime physician to George III. It is said that

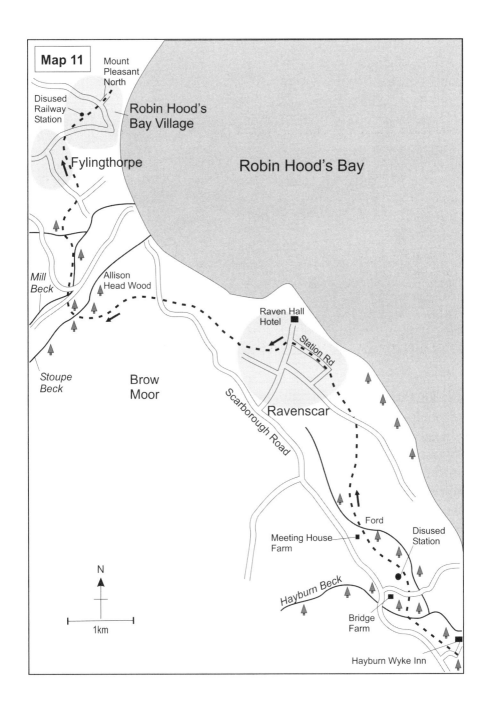

Map 11

Mount Pleasant North

Disused Railway Station

Robin Hood's Bay Village

Fylingthorpe

Robin Hood's Bay

Mill Beck

Allison Head Wood

Raven Hall Hotel

Station Rd

Stoupe Beck

Brow Moor

Ravenscar

Scarborough Road

Ford

Meeting House Farm

Disused Station

N

Hayburn Beck

1km

Bridge Farm

Hayburn Wyke Inn

Station Square at Ravenscar

the king came to Peak Hall to be treated for one of his regular bouts of madness, so as to keep him away from the public gaze. The hall changed hands following a wager on a race between two woodlice! The later owners added the crenellations, and it was subsequently turned into a hotel with pretty gardens situated at the edge of the cliffs, offering dramatic views down to the sea below.

With the coming of the railway in the 1880s, an ambitious scheme was devised to turn the village into a new holiday resort. The developers believed that the proximity of the sea and the new transport links would mean that the village would become popular with visitors, and could become a new tourist centre. The land was bought up, new roads laid out, and the area parcelled out into plots for sale to the public. Unfortunately, the scheme foundered because of the difficulties of reaching the sea down a very steep cliff path, whilst the exposed location on the top of the cliffs did not help either. The developers eventually went into liquidation with only a dozen properties sold. The evidence of the speculative boom can be seen in the remains of a ghostly road layout which leads to nothing more than empty, windswept fields.

The village today has seen a small revival in its fortunes due to its position on the Cleveland Way and as the eastern end of the Lyke Wake Walk. The area to the north of the hotel is now under the control of the National Trust and is a popular venue for walkers.

Looping down the track to Robin Hood's Bay

From Ravenscar, the disused railway track can be joined again quite easily by turning left at the Raven Hall Hotel down the main road which leads away from the coast. Almost immediately you will see a concrete path sloping off downhill to the right, with a sign indicating Robin Hood's Bay and Whitby. There is a National Park shop here on the right of the path if you want to stock up with supplies, or maybe just to buy an ice-cream.

You cycle down here for a few yards, and the path becomes a little less smooth, with disused bricks being used to provide the road surface. Very soon there is a fork at which you take the left-hand track, indicated as a cycle route. From here the route is clear, and you cycle on a cinder track with the remains of a huge quarry looming up on your left-hand side and shale tips everywhere. The going here is quite easy and there are some stunning views of Robin Hood's Bay in the distance, which you may want to stop and admire. Conveniently the route is provided with benches to sit on and admire the view, and I certainly found myself taking advantage of this opportunity.

The track then pulls round to the left and follows the contours of Brow Moor for about a mile, with many chances to see more dramatic views of the coast. Much of the route here is downhill and the cycling is often exhilarating, with your speed continually increasing as you speed down the track. The route continues downhill through a deep cutting, around a large loop of heavily-wooded land, which is part of Alison Head Wood. I found that I was now cycling so fast that it was too difficult to see what I was passing; I was just concentrating on what lay ahead on the route in case I bumped into anyone or anything!

After this, the route heads north in a series of slight curves along a part-wooded track towards Robin Hood's Bay. There are sporadic views of the sea and a glorious vista of Robin Hood's Bay through the trees, its myriad red roofs reflecting the sun. On the route you pass the disused station at Fyling Hall, with its whitewashed building and the sign on the gate saying 'Station

Bridge on the disused Scarborough to Whitby Line

Master', as if the line had never been closed, and you still expected to see the Station Master emerging hurriedly to meet the train. I found this part of the coastal route to be the best, with the advantage of a downhill slope for most of the time, and plenty of opportunities to appreciate the view of the coast – all cycle rides should be like this!

The cycleway eventually levels out and runs along towards the outskirts of Robin Hood's Bay, passing a caravan park on the left. Shortly after this, the route meets a major road running down into the village. At this point you need to turn right, and then take the next path off to the left at a sign indicating 'Village Hall'. There is also a sign indicating that this is the 'Cinder Trail'. The route runs up a slope and comes into the site of the old Robin Hood's Bay railway station, which is now the main car park for the village (947 055).

Robin Hood's Bay is a delightful village of red-roofed houses, which seems to almost tumble into the sea. There are many twisty lanes to explore, as well as the possibility of visiting some of the innumerable cafés and teahouses opened to cater for the tourist trade. However, you should note that the road down into the village is very steep for most of the way, and you may find it difficult, almost suicidal, to cycle down – and impossible to cycle back up! You might prefer to walk with your bike for most of the way, if you intend to go down to the bay itself.

The village developed as a key fishing port, but in the 18th-century it became infamous for its smuggling activities. The small, covered King's Beck stream led to a number of hidden trapdoors, giving access to local properties. It was said that contraband could be moved from the entrance of the beck right to the top of the village, without it ever seeing the light of day. The smuggling trade was very lucrative, and most of the inhabitants were complicit in this activity. In the 19th

A backward glance at Robin Hood's Bay

century, fishing took over as the main source of income, but this gradually declined to be replaced by tourism in more recent times. The village was a very close community in the past and few people would marry anyone outside of the village, with the result that a few local names predominated. Weddings and funerals were impressive affairs involving nearly everyone in the village, and effectively turning into local festivals.

The most puzzling feature about the village is its name. In the 16th-century the settlement was simply called 'Baytown', but the name 'Robin Hood's Bay' appeared soon after. There is no obvious connection with the historical Robin Hood, who lived many miles to the south. It is more likely that the name came from the many legends linked to his name which grew up afterwards. One such legend has Robin defeating a band of French pirates and distributing their booty to the poor people of the village. Whatever the truth of this story, the village is certainly worth a visit, and you might even see some of the 'Coast to Coast' walkers washing their feet in the North Sea to signify the end of their long journey.

Round the coast to Whitby Abbey

To continue on the route, you cycle along past the car park and out onto the main road leading into the village. This you cross, and go down the road opposite, called Mount Pleasant North (see Map 12). You will again see the signs indicating the 'Cinder Track' which are normally black with white writing. At the end of this road turn sharp left to regain the cycleway. Do not take the path off at the end of the road, as this is not a cycle route but the Cleveland Way path. The cycle way is obvious once you turn left at the end of the road, as it is clearly indicated as a cycle route.

The route then follows around a grand loop close to the coast with spectacular views over the sea. At this point the cycling is uphill for a while, which is unusual after Ravenscar, and the cycleway is often on an embankment. The track eventually straightens out and runs in a north-westerly direction towards the village of Hawsker (925 077), about two miles beyond Robin Hood's Bay. As you progress westwards, the skyline of Whitby finally comes into view with its towering abbey on the nearby headland. I felt uplifted when I first saw the outline of the abbey on the horizon, as I realised that the end of this stage was in sight – yet I also felt a little disappointed that this dramatic part of the route was over so quickly – sometimes we just cannot be satisfied! Shortly after, you pass a caravan park, and the whole of Whitby now appears, so that your final destination is clear. However, we now start to wheel away from the coast and head towards Hawsker Village.

View from viaduct over Esk near Whitby

You skirt past the edge of Hawsker and cross the A171 leading to Whitby, using the bridleway crossing provided. Note that the sign on the crossing shows a green horse, not a bike, when it is safe to cross! This is presumably because the cycle route is also a bridleway. Just beyond the crossing there is a cycle-hire shop, with a disused railway carriage being used to store the bikes, yet another way in which the disused stations on the line are being put to good use.

The cycle route runs parallel to the main road for a few minutes before reaching the edge of Stainsacre village (914 085), when it strikes off westwards to brush the edge of Cock Mill Wood. After a pleasant downhill run of about a mile through a leafy, shaded corridor, the track bends slightly to the right, before crossing over the River Esk by way of a monumental viaduct. You must take time

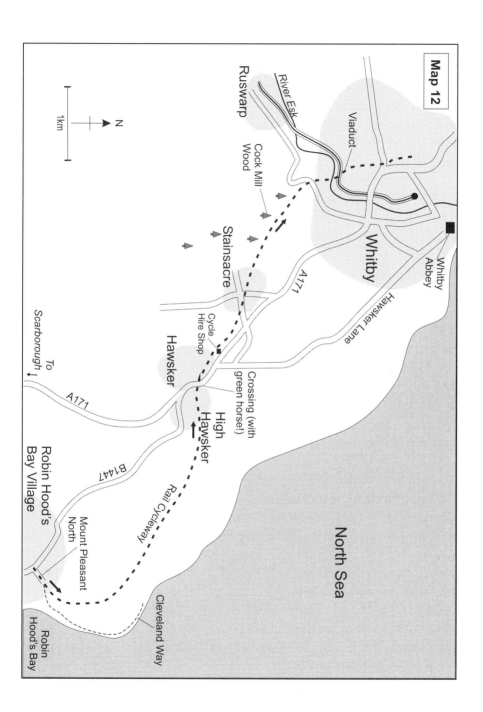

Map 12

Ruswarp

River Esk

Viaduct

Cock Mill
Wood

Stainsacre

Whitby

Whitby
Abbey

Hawsker Lane

A171

Cycle
Hire Shop

Hawsker

Crossing (with
green horse!)

To
Scarborough

A171

High
Hawsker

Rail Cycleway

North Sea

B1447

Robin Hood's
Bay Village

Mount Pleasant
North

Cleveland Way

Robin
Hood's Bay

N

1km

to look at this marvellous structure, and admire the views over Whitby and the River Esk nestled below. If you are lucky, as I was, you might even see a steam train far below on the Esk Valley line, coming into Whitby on the other side of the river, looking like a toy train from a train set. I felt that this stunning view over the Esk Valley and the town of Whitby was a fitting end to this spectacular part of the journey.

On the other side of the viaduct you enter the suburbs of Whitby, where you leave the cycleway, and cycle into the town itself. However, at first, just continue along the track, which soon runs into an enclosed section of the route, sandwiched between high embankments. Shortly after passing under a large bridge, with creeper-like vegetation hanging below, you will come to a litter bin with a blue cycle-route indicator pointing to an exit off to the left. Take this path, which slopes down quickly to the tarmac road below, and then turn sharp right to go under a bridge, which carries the Cinder Track a few more yards into Whitby. Follow the road, and you will soon come to a busy roundabout, at which you should go straight ahead. This road leads down into town, and within a few minutes you will be at the town centre next to the railway station and the harbour area.

The town of Whitby grew up around a natural harbour, which offered the best berthing facilities between the Tyne and the Humber, until the development of Teesside. For most of that time Whitby was also a major religious centre, following the founding of the Abbey in 656 AD by Hilda, the daughter of King Oswy of Northumbria. The town was the venue for the famous Synod of Whitby in 664 AD, at which the decision was made to adopt the Catholic rather than the Celtic form of Christianity. The Abbey was destroyed by the Vikings in 867 AD, but was rebuilt in the later 11th-century, and its remains still rise high above the promontory on the east side of the river Esk, visible from many miles away.

Whitby flourished in the 17th and 18th centuries as a fishing centre and major port. The town imported coal used to produce the alum for dyeing cloth, and it also exported fish. Whaling became a major activity from the 1750s with Whitby becoming a centre for the processing and export of whale oil, used for fuel in lamps. In addition, Whitby began to produce articles made out of a locally-mined mineral called 'Jet', which was popular in the 19th-century. The evidence for this period of prosperity can be seen in the terraces of fine Georgian houses to be found on the west cliff.

The town today is mainly a tourist centre, although a healthy inshore fishing industry still survives. If time allows, you should wander around the narrow streets on the east bank of the town, and climb the 199 steps up to the abbey at the top of the hill. The steps were originally made of wood, and until the mid-19th-century there were no railings to prevent the weary traveller from falling to his death. Parallel to the steps is a steep road called 'the old donkey road' which also leads up to the top of the hill, but you would find it difficult to get any vehicle up there today!

You can visit St. Mary's church next to the abbey, which was extensively refitted in the 18th-century with wooden pews and galleries, and you may note it has a very 'nautical' feel inside. Nearby is Abbey House, which was erected by the Cholmley Family in the mid-17th-century using stone taken from the abbey. The house was extensively extended in the 18th-century, but was badly damaged in a gale in 1800 before being renovated by its new owners, the Strickland Family, who were also the Lords of the Manor of Whitby.

The graveyard at the top of the hill is windswept and atmospheric, so it is no surprise that it was the inspiration for one of the settings in Bram Stoker's 'Dracula'. Today the town plays host to an annual 'Goth' festival in which people throng the town, dressed in black clothes and makeup. As one of the smaller tourist resorts, Whitby has plenty of places to stay, and of course many pubs and cafés to provide much-needed refreshments.

5: Riding the Ironstone Railway

Day 5	Whitby to Lord Stones (Maps 13-16)
Distance	28 Miles
Allow	6 hours
Terrain	This is an easy route at the start, but then has long climbs over the moors and a strenuous section on the Ironstone Railway. The end section is quite rough at times as you skirt the northern escarpment
Toilets	Grosmont, Rosedale, Blakey Inn, Lord Stones
Refreshments	Pubs at Rosedale, the Lion Inn at Blakey, cafés at Rosedale and Lord Stones

An easy run along Esk Dale

The final leg of the journey is one of the longest stretches, but at the same time one of the most rewarding. It covers a wide range of landscapes, from sleepy valleys to the top of the moors, and alongside the northern face of the Cleveland hills. It contains a number of memorable features, such as the old Rosedale Ironstone railway line, and the sharp descents of the 'Incline' and the 'Chimney', as well as the welcoming sight of the 'Lion Inn' at Blakey, and ultimately Lord Stones Café, for the second and final time.

You start the route by retracing your steps out of Whitby to re-join the railway viaduct (see Map 13). To do this, just take the road that leads up from the station and go straight ahead at the mini roundabout. This leads to a minor road which soon passes under a railway arch with the name 'Cinder Track' on a red sign. Go under the arch and immediately turn left, as this is the cycle access route

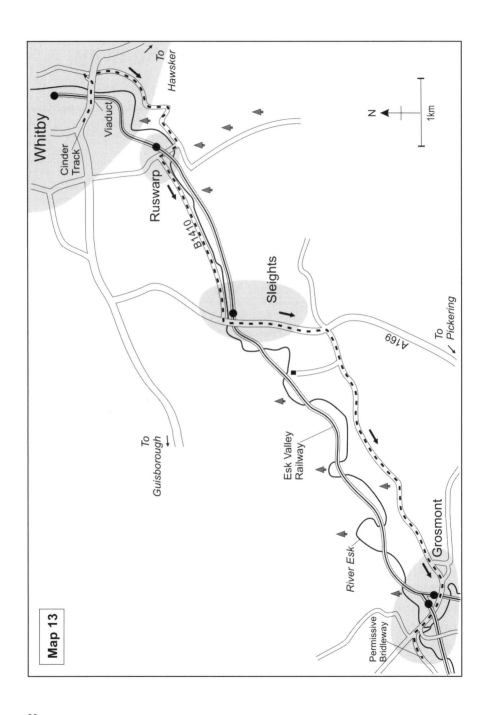

Map 13

90

you came down earlier. Then keep to the left-hand path and this will take you up to the disused railway track. Follow the track until it re-crosses the viaduct, and then take the first turning off to the left, then sharply to the right and you will come to the road which runs between Whitby and Ruswarp.

You turn right onto this road and cycle towards Ruswarp for about ½ mile until you come to a junction with the river Esk on your right-hand side. Here, turn right and go over the metal girder bridge which crosses the Esk, and then continue over the railway level-crossing adjacent to the station. Immediately after crossing the railway is a junction at which you should turn left, and you then head into the village of Ruswarp.

Ruswarp (pronounced "Russup"), is a lively little village, located on the river Esk, just west of Whitby. The village has long been a popular place for visitors due to the development of a number of tourist attractions. In the 19th-century, the Glen Esk woodlands just to the south-east of the village were a popular beauty spot, centred around the impressive Cock Mill waterfall with its 35-foot cascade.

In more recent times other attractions have opened in Ruswarp itself. At Ruswarp Pleasure Boats, it is possible to hire a boat or canoe and take it up river as far as the River Gardens Café, about a mile upstream. The river here is quite slow-flowing and so it is not too difficult to do this, and then to allow the current to bring you back. In addition, for young children, there is a miniature railway which occasionally has steam trains running at the weekends. Other attractions have also been located here in the past, including a putting green and 'Monster' ride. It seems that a virtual pleasure park, which still awaits discovery, has been created in this unassuming location.

You leave Ruswarp along the B1410, which runs by the river for 1½ miles to Sleights. This is a very easy ride, right next to the riverbank, and you may well see some holidaymakers struggling with their rowing boats in the middle of the river. About a mile down the road, it is possible to get refreshments at the previously mentioned River Garden Café, which is just before you get to Sleights. This is a café in an excellent garden centre, which is open every day from 10.00am, and is situated on the banks of the Esk, allowing you to sit by the side of the river and take in the peace of the countryside. My advice is to stop here a while and enjoy this relaxed start to the ride; the route starts to get more difficult as we continue!

The word Sleights rhymes with 'nights' and the name means 'flat land near water'. As such, this seems rather a misnomer, as the village actually hugs the side of the A169 as it plunges down into the Esk valley, and then rises steeply up to the moors on the south side of the valley.

The village is the largest in the North York Moors and many of the houses are quite modern. Indeed, the village looks more like a suburb of Whitby than a moorland village, and it is likely that most of its inhabitants are actually commuters. The village has a wide variety of shops and cafés along the main road and it is certainly a good place to stock up with supplies.

At the junction of the B1410 with the A169, turn left and go south until you come to the 'B' road from Sleights to Grosmont on the other side of the river. To reach this, however, you need to follow the A169 main road through Sleights for about a mile. This is an uphill route on a busy through road and you might find it easier to walk part of the way – I certainly did. Eventually you turn off to the right at a signposted road, just after a building with a clock in the gable end, opposite a small cemetery (866 068).

Although it is rather hard work to get to the turn-off, I think it is well worthwhile. The road to Grosmont is an undulating road of about three miles, which offers splendid views over the Esk valley, passing by many immaculately kept cottage gardens. Cycling down this road, early in the day, I felt I had a grandstand view of Esk Dale, with the road running along the side of the slopes which lead to Sleights Moor. In the distance, I could just make out the little clouds of steam rising into the air from the trains at Grosmont station. Suddenly the road began to drop down sharply, and in no time I was speeding down the hill into Grosmont, leading me to the hustle and bustle of this picturesque railway junction.

Grosmont is a small village which lies in a deep valley formed by the Murk Esk, a tributary of the Esk River. The village was a centre for iron-making in the late 19th-century, using locally-mined ores. There was an iron works and blast furnaces, as well as a brickworks. At that time the village was simply referred to as 'Tunnel' after the tunnel, next to the village, through which the railway ran . It later changed its name to Grosmont, this referring to a 13th-century priory which was founded by French monks, none of which remains.

The village is now more peaceful, and rural in nature. However, today it houses the engine-sheds for the North Yorkshire Moors Railway. If you make a short diversion, you can see the trains being repaired and refitted. This can be done by cycling down the path adjacent to the railway line heading to Pickering. You go over a metal bridge and then through the disused mid-19th-century railway tunnel, and immediately you come out at the entrance to the engine sheds.

The station is a busy junction, linking up with the Esk Valley Railway. It is quite an enjoyable experience, just spending some time on the platform watching the trains come and go. In addition you can get a welcome snack at the railway station if you need sustenance at this stage.

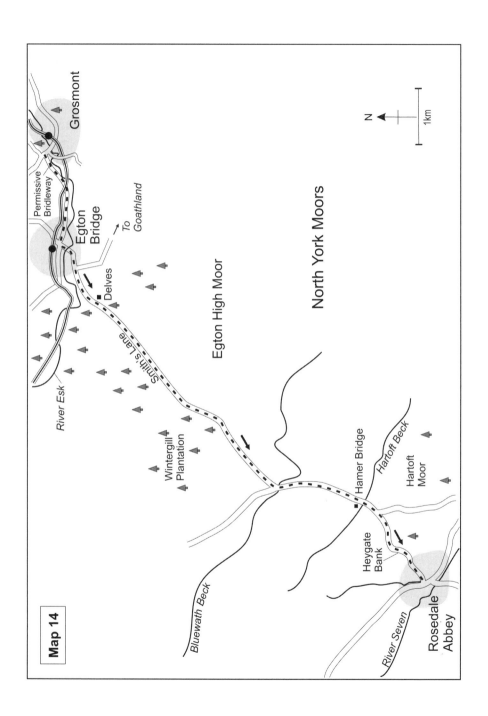

Map 14

Grosmont

Permissive Bridleway

Egton Bridge

To Goathland

River Esk

Delves

Smith's Lane

Egton High Moor

North York Moors

Wintergill Plantation

Hamer Bridge

Hartoft Beck

Hartoft Moor

Heygate Bank

Bluewath Beck

River Seven

Rosedale Abbey

N

1km

You now need to take the road westwards out of Grosmont, passing under the railway bridge and then turning right to head north for about ½ mile before crossing over a narrow bridge. You then bear to the right, and will come across a bridleway off to your left a few yards along the road (824 055). This is the old Barnard's Road toll road and it is a permissive bridleway for the use of cyclists, horse riders and walkers (see Map 14). The bridleway to Egton Bridge offers a nice, relatively smooth ride, along a slightly sloping track which crosses under the railway, eventually coming out next to Egton Bridge station. On the way, it passes Toll Booth Cottage, where the toll booth was located. A copy of the toll charges is displayed on a wooden board at the far side of the cottage and is well worth a quick glance before you cycle on. I found this little track quite idyllic to ride along, running along just next to the river Esk, and ending by the grounds of the manor house at Egton Bridge. More to the point, it is the last bit of easy riding before the hard climb up to Egton High Moors begins – so my advice is to enjoy it while it lasts!

Over Egton Moor

At the junction at the end of the bridleway, you turn left and follow the 'B' road which runs south to Goathland. This turns sharp right, and crosses the river over a bridge rebuilt in 1993, after the original one was swept away by floodwater. Shortly after, you take the minor road off right to Rosedale, which continues onwards up a gradually-increasing slope to the small settlement at Delves (792 046). This was a place I remember well, as the site of my only puncture on the entire circuit! The road then winds steeply up the bank until it reaches Egton High Moor, where it straightens out. The going here was quite hard with the road seeming to stretch on into the distance, going upwards for ever. At times I resorted to pushing my bike up the road, with the sun blazing down on me, as the moor gradually came into view ahead. By the time I started to saddle up and ride again, I could see that I had gained a lot of height from the valley below, but it had been quite an effort.

The road crosses Hamer Moor, past a series of disused coal workings, and eventually drops down to the deserted hamlet of Hamer Bridge (743 977), nestling in Hartoft Beck. Once there was a pub on this river crossing, but this has long since been abandoned and the place seems rather eerie. The route rises again sharply at the other side of the beck, and passes over Hartoft Moor, after which it descends again to the village of Rosedale Abbey (725 959), this now being on the Outdoor Leisure Map Western Area (Explorer OL 26). From the top of Hartoft Moor it is just possible to see the buildings next to the 'Lion Inn' at Blakey in the distance, a sure sign that you are making progress. I found this a very heartening sight, and I began to feel that I was nearly home, as the Lion marks the start of the railway route to the 'Ingleby Incline' and down into the Tees Valley. From here, the sharp descent to Rosedale Abbey down Heygate Bank offers an excellent opportunity to rest your weary legs, and let gravity do the work, whilst also providing you with an exciting ride. At the end of the road you speed into the little village of Rosedale Abbey, where you should take the opportunity to have a well-deserved rest.

The village of Rosedale Abbey is named after a 12th-century Cistercian priory, which was once situated in this secluded valley. The priory was established in 1154, probably founded as a Benedictine house, but it later appears to have links to the Cistercian Order. The priory was never large in size, but it did have an important impact on the community, developing the export of woollen goods to Italy and running some forty farms. It was also a centre of charitable activity, providing a place for travellers to stay. The priory was closed down at the dissolution of the monasteries, and most of the stone was re-used for other buildings. The ruins of the priory have now almost entirely disappeared. Only the remains of one of the stone stair-turrets still remains in the grounds of the parish church, but there is a selection of carved windows and stones from the priory, which are now incorporated into the brickwork of several other properties in the village.

Rosedale Abbey remains

In the 16th-century Rosedale became famous for the manufacture of glassware. This was produced by Huguenot glass workers who had fled from religious conflict in France. They produced the glass clandestinely, in furnaces on the side of Spaunton moor, some way outside the village. This was because the manufacture of glass at that time was controlled by a royal monopoly and as the Huguenot refugees could not get permission to make glass legally, they resorted to making it illegally in remote locations. It appears that the activity ended very suddenly after only a few decades, suggesting that the whereabouts of the furnaces became known to the authorities. In recent years a local glassware outlet has opened in the village selling goods to the tourists.

In the 19th-century, the valley became the centre of a new kind of industrial activity, with the discovery of ironstone deposits. This was mined locally and the ore was 'roasted' in huge kilns to remove the water and other impurities. The ore was then shipped across to the iron workings in the Tees valley by way of the Rosedale Ironstone Railway, the abandoned track of which now provides a major part of the cycle route on the final part of the Cleveland Circular.

In more recent days the industry has disappeared, but Rosedale has become a popular watering place for walkers and cyclists, with a wide variety of places to stop and get refreshments. Apart from various pubs there are a number of cafés, such as the Abbey Tea Rooms and the Graze on the Grass Tea Shop, both of which have attractive tea

Rosedale ironstone kilns

gardens. There are also some useful public conveniences which are very new and well -maintained.

However, cyclists should soon be ready to press on to the 'Lion Inn' at Blakey if they want to make progress; there is still a long way to go! You follow the 'B' road south out of the village for a few yards, before turning off to the right on the road to Hutton-le-Hole (see Map 15). This minor road leads to the infamous Chimney Bank, an exceptionally steep road, which winds like a corkscrew out of the Rosedale Valley. This is named after a chimney stack from the engine house, which was used to haul ironstone up to the railway track at the top of the bank. The chimney stood some 50 feet high at the top of the bank and was demolished in about 1970.

The road up the bank was used in the early 20th-century as a location for motorcycle trials. At that time the road was even steeper, with gradients of up to 40%, and the road surface was not tarmac as it is today. Even now, the road seems impossibly steep as it spirals out of Rosedale up to the top of the moors. Very determined cyclists might try to cycle up here to prove how fit they are. I knew how fit I was, so I walked up instead, pushing my bike along with me!

Nearly at the top, there is an interesting set of ironstone kilns which can be visited, and a seat opposite which offers a welcome rest. Just beyond, you come across the track of the old Rosedale Ironstone Railway where it crosses the road (721 946). You then turn right along the disused rail track, heading northwards in the direction of the valley head for about 3 miles.

The Rosedale Ironstone Railway
The 14-mile Rosedale Ironstone Railway is one of the most impressive man-made features encountered on the route. This was a railway which linked the iron mines in the Rosedale Valley to the iron works in Teesside, crossing over the top of Farndale Moor and Westerdale

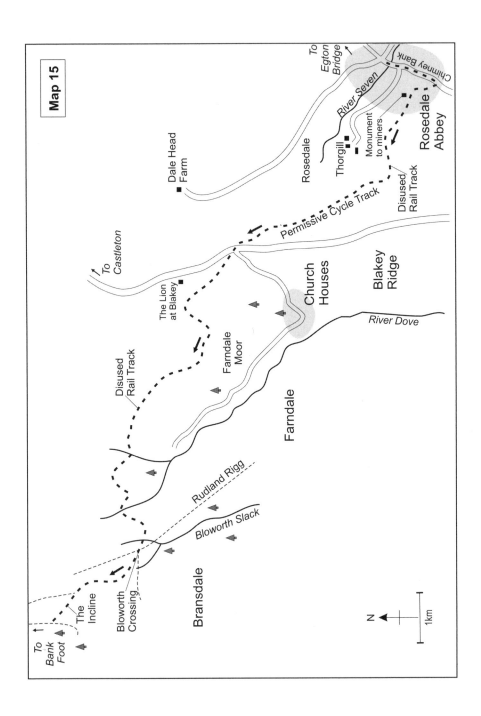

Map 15

To Egton Bridge

Chimney Bank

River Seven

Rosedale Abbey

Dale Head Farm

Rosedale

Thorgill

Monument to miners

Disused Rail Track

Permissive Cycle Track

To Castleton

The Lion at Blakey

Church Houses

Blakey Ridge

River Dove

Disused Rail Track

Farndale Moor

Farndale

Rudland Rigg

Bloworth Slack

Bransdale

The Incline

Bloworth Crossing

To Bank Foot

N

1km

100

Moor, before running down the steep 'Ingleby Incline' to the junction at Battersby. The railway is a feat of Victorian engineering, running for much of its length at an altitude of over 1000 feet, crossing bleak, windswept moorland. In its heyday, the route was covered with winding houses, railway sheds and workshops, providing employment for many local people.

The railway was constructed following the discovery of valuable ironstone deposits in the Rosedale valley, which was worked by the Rosedale Mining Company. Originally, the ironstone was shipped out to the ironworks of the north-east by way of a circuitous route south, through Pickering and Malton. However, in 1861 the mining company financed the construction of a railway over the moors, to meet up with the newly-opened railway which ran from Stokesley to Kildale via Battersby Junction. The Rosedale Ironstone Railway originally served the Rosedale West mines, but a branch line was created to link up with the Rosedale East mines four years later. The future of the railway became uncertain with the gradual decline and closure of the Rosedale mines, hit by competition from cheaper, imported ores. The last mines closed in 1926, and the final train ran down the Rosedale railway in 1929.

Most of the track runs on a level across the moors, curving around the top of Farndale and Westerdale before running eastwards onto Blakey Ridge, which separates Farndale from Rosedale. Here it runs under the road from Hutton-le-Hole to Castleton close to the Lion Inn. After running under the road, the track runs off to the ironstone mines in Rosedale, with a short spur off to the Blakey mine just before running under the road.

The track was designed for goods transport, but it was also used by local people as a quick means of travelling from Rosedale to the Tees Valley. In particular it provided an efficient means of getting from Rosedale to the Stokesley show. In many ways, the demise of the railway has meant that the inhabitants of Rosedale are now more cut off from Teesside than they were 100 years ago. Nowadays, the disused track provides an excellent bridleway, much frequented by walkers, cyclists and horse riders.

The section from Rosedale Bank Top to the tarmac road along Blakey Ridge is a permissive cycle track, and the owners (Spaunton Estates) are happy for cyclists to use it so long as they give way to walkers. In addition, all users should respect the needs of gamekeepers and shepherds who work there, as the area is a working farm estate. Indeed the same could be said for all of the disused railway line where it crosses the moorland area.

The route is easy to cycle and offers excellent views across the valley, where you can just make out another branch of the route running past a series of abandoned workings. The whole of the valley-head opens up in front of you, and I found that the section up to the Lion was like an upland version of the route I had cycled some time before towards Grosmont.

A short distance along the track I came across an intriguing monument to the ironstone miners, which is worth stopping to look at. The inscriptions on the two sides read as follows;

> *'In the dark, working hard, loading up the wooden cart'* and the other side says *'Work shift over, in the sun, on the hill, having fun'.*

This is a monument erected about 10 years ago to commemorate the miners who worked in the ironstone mines. The monument was the result of collaboration between a local sculptor and the children of Rosedale Primary School. It was the children who actually came up with the design of the piece and the words written on it. It is a fitting tribute to the many miners who toiled in this area in the past, enduring many hardships.

Eventually the track meets a short path off to the left which leads onto a nearby road. This is the minor road along Blakey Ridge, which runs along to the 'Lion Inn' at Blakey and a welcome break if you have not yet stopped. Once you join the road, turn right up the slope and cycle about ¼ mile along the road to the top of the hill, when the pub comes into view on the left-hand side.

The Lion Inn (679 997), stands on the top of Blakey Ridge, one the highest and most remote parts of the North York Moors, at an altitude of nearly 1300 feet. Although there are few local inhabitants now, in the 19th-century there were large numbers of miners who lived nearby in the Rosedale and Farndale Valleys. Apart from ironstone mines, there were also coal pits on the moors to the north, as well as workers on the railway, so the area was much more heavily populated than it is today. Now most of the clientele consists of day trippers, walkers on the Lyke Wake Walk, or cyclists on the many moorland routes. It is the tourist trade which now keeps the Lion Inn busy, and it is certainly worthwhile stopping here to sample the wide variety of local beers and to fill up with a hot or cold lunch.

However, you must not delay too long, as the last section of the circuit now awaits you. If you want to miss out the pub (such determined people!) you just cross over the road along Blakey Ridge, go down the steeply-sloping road on the far side which goes to Farndale, and turn off to the right shortly after at the rail track.

This last section begins with a continuation of the abandoned Rosedale Ironstone Railway, which will eventually lead back to the Tees Valley. Like most railway routes, the way is mainly flat, with the track meandering at the edge of High Blakey Moor, following the various gills that feed into Farndale. The views over the dales are extensive, and I found that they took my mind off the monotony of the track itself, as I basked in the warmth of the summer sun (I was lucky with the weather!).

After about three miles, the route eventually comes out onto a short, straight section, where it is crossed by the ancient track along Rudland Rigg at Blowarth Crossing (617 014). This was an important junction in the past and the level crossing was controlled by a gatekeeper, whose house once stood on this exposed site. From this point you can also see into the wooded valley of Bransdale, which runs just to the west of Farndale. You are now at the watershed of the North York Moors, with the steep-sided northern escarpments only a few hundred yards away. It is to this dramatic drop, with its breathtaking views, that you now continue.

Beyond Blowarth Crossing you turn round an arc to the right, and suddenly the Cleveland plain comes into view. Shortly afterwards, you reach the top of the 'Ingleby Incline', a steep slope down which the railway track used to descend to Battersby Junction. The views over the Cleveland plain from the top of the incline are truly magnificent, with the villages and towns of the Tees Valley spread out before you, as if on a gigantic green tablecloth. Surely this can claim to be one of the best views in the north of England, and a superb climax to the whole of the journey. For the daring cyclist, this is the start of a rapid descent at breakneck speed to the bottom of the slope, taking care to stop at the fence halfway down! Myself, I tended to make liberal use of my brakes – maybe I am just not daring enough!

The Ingleby Incline runs for 1430 yards, rising from 600 to 1370 feet to reach the top of Greenhow Bank, achieving a maximum gradient of 1 in 5. The railway here operated as a self-acting incline railway, by which loaded wagons running down the incline helped to pull up the unloaded wagons on an adjacent track. This was achieved by using a large drum, around which a one-inch-diameter cable was wound, attached to the descending wagons. Another drum was attached to the same drive shaft, so that as the first drum rotated, it also rotated the second drum. This hauled up the empty wagons on the adjacent

Looking down Ingleby incline (Photograph Andrew Wright)

track. The whole operation was controlled by two operators in a brake cabin at the top of the incline. The incline was not wooded then, so they had a clear view of the line below. However, this did not prevent serious accidents, especially when the wagons broke away from the cables.

A final run by the northern escarpment

At the bottom of the slope, you turn sharp left to take the wooded path at the base of the escarpment (see Map 16). This pleasant winding road threads through the Greenhow Plantation for about 1½ miles, before meeting the minor road, which plunges down from Clay Bank to Ingleby Greenhow. At last I started to feel that the hard cycling was done and the end was in sight. The views over

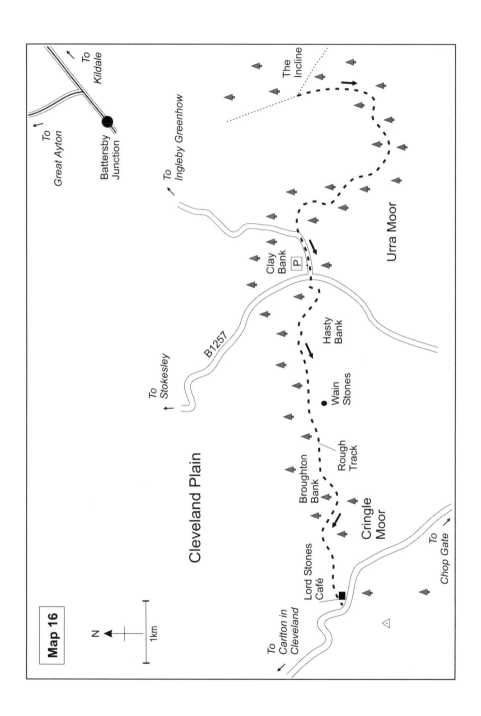

Map 16

N

1km

To
Great Ayton

To
Kildale

Battersby
Junction

The
Incline

To
Ingleby Greenhow

Urra Moor

Clay
Bank

P

Hasty
Bank

Cleveland Plain

To
Stokesley

B1257

Wain
Stones

Rough
Track

Broughton
Bank

Cringle
Moor

Lord Stones
Café

To
Carlton in
Cleveland

To
Chop Gate

the valley were enchanting, with the little farmsteads of the Cleveland plain picked out in the bright sunlight below.

At the junction with the road, you turn left up the hill, and very soon you will reach the car-park at Clay Bank (573 034). There are wonderful views over the Cleveland Plain from the car-park, and sometimes a mobile café selling refreshments, but no toilets. For reasons which are beyond me, there is no permanent café here – I am sure it would be very popular.

The final few miles involve skirting the lower slopes of the northern escarpment of the Cleveland Hills, a route providing fine views, if tricky-going at times. From Clay Bank, the route re-starts at the other side of the B1257, the main road from Stokesley to Helmsley, where a short path through the woods over a number of tree-roots leads to a muddy forestry track. Turn left up a steep slope which curves gradually to the right and soon you come out into the open, by a seat next to a dry-stone wall. On the other side of the wall, a steep path leads to the summit of the escarpment at Hasty Bank. However, you continue straight on by the right-hand side of the wall along a boulder-strewn route, with the north face of Hasty Bank looming up above, and the woods of the Greenhow Plantation just below. The rough track gradually improves, and becomes a pleasant wooded path running parallel to the line of the hills, with occasional views through the trees on your right to the plains below.

It is a marvellous experience to ride along this wooded path, although you do have to watch yourself at times as the slope on your right can be quite precipitous. The route becomes a little rocky again, as it comes out of the wood and approaches Broughton Bank. Here there is a relatively steep descent and you may have to dismount. The track eventually leads to a gate, just before the stream at the bottom of the bank, and then continues on an easier path at the other side before leading onto a short stretch of paved pathway. Just beyond this point, there is a signpost which indicates the bridleway leading off the right, with the looming presence of Cringle Moor in front of you.

The track on the north side of Cringle Moor is more difficult than the previous stretch in front of Hasty Bank, as much of the area is used as a testing cycling-track for daredevil mountain bikers. The trick is to keep to the higher ground, so as to avoid coming across sudden descents to the bottom of the slope. The higher route is clearly waymarked, and will take you past a mound of spoil, before leading to a rapidly-undulating track, which weaves up and down along the slopes of Busby Moor. This is an exhilarating ride and a

Forestry Road at the bottom of the Incline

fitting finale to the Cleveland Circular. With good luck and judgement, you will finally reach a small wooden gate, which leads down a rough track and eventually comes out onto the grassy slopes above Lord Stones Café (523 030).

At last the end is in sight. The track leads down the slope to a signpost where you turn sharp left along the bridleway up a slight slope along the side of the hill. The track runs a hundred yards or so to reach a wooden gate, where you turn right down a steep track paved with stone slabs. This levels out onto a wide grassy path which soon brings you to the welcome sight of Lord Stones café. After such a gruelling final stage, the sense of achievement is so much greater. The relieved cyclist can gradually freewheel the last few yards to the café and enjoy some welcome refreshments. The circuit is complete, the journey done!

Bibliography

Books

Boyes, M. & Chester, H. 1996. *Discovering the North York Moors*. Otley: Smith Settle Ltd.

Fletcher, R. 2003. *St. Gregory's Minster Kirkdale*. The Trustees of the Friends of St. Gregory's Minster, Kirkdale.

In Search of Rosedale Glass. 1997. North York Moors National Park.

Lidster, J. Robin 2010. *The Scarborough and Whitby Railway*. Amberley Publishing

Morrison, J. 2007. *AA Mini Guide to the North York Moors*. Basingstoke: AA Publishing

North Yorkshire Railway Guide Book. 2012 . North Yorkshire Moors Railway.

Rhodes, Simon M. 1997. *Ravenscar. The town that never was*. Scarborough: Smart Publications.

Seekings, K. 2005. *Rosedale Abbey: The Story of a Medieval Nuns' Priory 1154-1536*. United Benefice of Lastingham Occasional Papers

Spencer, B. 2011. *North York Moors (Landmark Visitors Guide)*. Ashbourne: The Horizon Press

Websites

Ravenscar and Staintondale Stories (www.coastaltourism.co.uk)

Rosedale Mines and Tramway by Roy Lambeth in Subterranea Brittanica (www.subbrit.org.uk)

A Short History and Introduction to Rosedale by Rosedale History Society (rosedalehistory@hotmail.co.uk)

Welcome to Lockton and Levisham by Lockton and Levisham Heritage Group (www.locktonlevisham.btck.co.uk)

Also from Sigma Leisure:

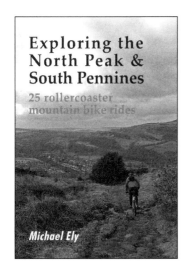

Exploring the North Peak & South Pennines
25 rollercoaster mountain bike rides
Michael Ely

This book will inspire you to pump up the tyres and oil the chain for some excitement, exercise and a feast of rollercoaster riding as you join Michael Ely on some great mountain biking in these Pennine hills. Over 500 miles of riding for the adventurous off-road cyclist that explore the tracks and steep lanes in the Pennine hills. There are twenty-five illustrated rides - with cafe stops half way round - to provide both a challenge and many hours of healthy exercise in classic mountain biking country.
£8.99

Ghost Walks around York
Over 50 of York's haunted locations
David Shaw

For over 20 years David Shaw has been a regular visitor to the beautiful and historic city of York and during his pleasant stays gradually became aware of the enormous wealth of reported ghost sightings in the area. The walks in this illustrated book include descriptions of hauntings in 60 locations.
£8.99

All-Terrain Pushchair Walks

The North York Moors

Zoë Sayer and Rebecca Terry

Explore the North York Moors — the perfect place to both keep fit and introduce your children to the delights of the outdoors. This fully revised and updated 2nd edition includes gradings and at-a-glance symbols to make walk choice easy and allow you to plan ahead. There are 30 walks spread across the entire national park from riverside walks and coastal strolls to rambles through the heather moors. £8.99

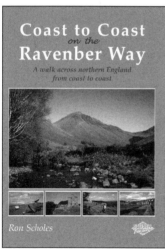

Coast to Coast

On the Ravenber Way

Ron Scholes

The walk described in the book follows existing rights of way in the form of footpaths, bridleways and tracks, making this cross-country route a challenging long-distance journey. The walk commences at Ravenglass, it passes Lakeland's finest array of high peaks, climbs over the high Pennines, traverses the northern moors and ends at Berwick-upon-Tweed. £9.99